U0022202

英語 Make Me High 系列

四版

108課綱、全民英檢中級適用

作文100隨身讀

三民英語編輯小組 彙整

三民書局

序

英語 Make Me High 系列的理想在於超越，在於創新。
這是時代的精神，也是我們出版的動力；
這是教育的目的，也是我們進步的執著。

針對英語的全球化與未來的升學趨勢，
我們設計了一系列適合普高、技高學生的英語學習書籍。

面對英語，不會徬徨不再迷惘，學習的心徹底沸騰，
心情好 High！
實戰模擬，掌握先機知己知彼，百戰不殆決勝未來，
分數更 High！

選擇優質的英語學習書籍，才能激發學習的強烈動機；
興趣盎然便不會畏懼艱難，自信心要自己大聲說出來。
本書如良師指引循循善誘，如益友相互鼓勵攜手成長。
展書輕閱，你將發現……
學習英語原來也可以這麼 High！

《 給讀者的話 》

　　聽、說、讀、寫這四種英文能力當中，就屬寫作最為複雜。想要寫出一些句子並不困難，任何上過英文課的學生皆可辦到。但是，若是想寫出一篇好的作文，這其中卻存在著很大的困難。

　　增進寫作技巧的方法很多，但一般認為，透過大量閱讀精采的好文章才能達到最好的效果。其實說穿了，寫作就是一段「模仿」的過程，藉由吸收別人文章的精華，長時間累積下來，自然而然就能透過自己的筆桿，寫出語意流暢且結構嚴謹的好文章。俗話說，「熟讀唐詩三百首，不會作詩也會吟」，就是這個道理。

　　本書所彙整的 100 篇作文範例，題材搜羅學測等大考及各校模擬考試作文題目，共分為三大部分：「看圖寫作」、「簡函寫作」和「主題寫作」。每篇字數符合大考規定範圍，篇篇皆為容易模仿上手的短文，十分適合讀者觀摩；輔以文章關鍵字詞解說，加上精闢的寫作建議，包括常見用法、常見句型、轉折語和連接詞等，教讀者如何下筆，以及可以套用在哪一類型的作文題目中。讀者可以一邊熟悉不同的寫作主題，一邊習得實用單字和片語，雙管齊下的功效，讓英文寫作功力日益精進。

　　本書之內容與編排力求完善，然則難免有疏漏之處，尚祈讀者不吝賜教。

三民英語編輯小組謹誌

本書收錄的歷年試題內容由財團法人大學入學考試中心基金會大學入學考試中心提供，試題著作權屬財團法人大學入學考試中心基金會所有。

本書圖片來源：Shutterstock

⟍ Table of Contents ╱

第三部分：主題寫作

1 Shopping

請仔細觀察以下三幅連環圖片的內容，並想像第四幅圖片可能的
發展，然後寫出一篇涵蓋每張圖片內容且結局完整的故事。

Shopping is one of Maggie's [1]favorite hobbies. She enjoys buying all kinds of [2]fashionable goods, [3]especially during the sales. Last weekend, she went to ABC Department Store because clothes there were [4]on sale. [5]As usual, she paid by [6]credit card. Then, she went home happily but almost couldn't open her door. There were too many shopping bags on the floor and behind the door.

When Maggie opened all the shopping bags, she realized that she had bought the same dress twice! Both were [7]name-brand dresses and had a floral [8]pattern. She was so surprised and started to ponder what to do. Suddenly, she thought of her best friend, Tina. Tina's birthday would be coming the next week, and she had wanted a floral dress for a long time. So, [9]instead of [10]returning this dress to the department store, Maggie decided the best way to solve the problem was to give the dress to Tina as her birthday present.

Total: 158 words

Vocabulary & Phrases in Use

1. **favorite** adj. 最喜愛的
2. **fashionable** adj. 流行的
3. **especially** adv. 尤其
4. **on sale** phr. 特價
5. **as usual** phr. 一如往常
6. **credit card** n. 信用卡
7. **name-brand** adj. 名牌的 (亦作 brand-name)
8. **pattern** n. 花樣
9. **instead of** prep. 作為…的替代
10. **return sth to sb** 把某物退還給某人

Writing Tips

1. 依照圖片編號的順序來發展故事，時態須前後一致，可以是現在式或過去式。

2. 寫作時須密切注意圖片情節的變化，清楚描述每一張圖片，例如運用時間副詞 last weekend 清楚標記時間的前後，並注意描述每張圖片的篇幅盡量平均，且合理解釋情節發展的來龍去脈。

3. 本文運用 a floral pattern 描述衣服上的花朵圖案，可套用在類似情境的文章中。

4. 本文有不少英文寫作中常見的用法，在本書其他文章中也會反覆出現，可學起來應用在作文中，例如用動名詞當作主詞 (Shopping is...)，以及逗點前後都指同一人的同位語 (...her best friend, Tina.)。還有表示時間的關係副詞 when (當…)，例如：When Maggie opened..., she realized that...，可在類似情境的文章中多加運用。

❷ Apology

請仔細觀察以下三幅連環圖片的內容，並想像第四幅圖片可能的
發展，然後寫出一篇涵蓋每張圖片內容且結局完整的故事。

Last Friday night, David celebrated [1]graduation with his
classmates. They went to a karaoke bar and sang together happily.
They were so happy that the party went on all night. When the party
was finally over, it was almost 4 a.m.! He said goodbye to his
classmates and took a taxi home. Once he got home, he [2]fell asleep
without [3]taking a shower.

The next day, David [4]overslept. When he finally woke up, he
found that he was late for the date with his girlfriend, Jenny. He felt
so bad that he ran all the way to meet her. When he got there, Jenny
was really angry and told him that she had waited for him for more
than two hours! David [5]apologized for being late. He [6]promised that
he would never [7]stay up so late as to [8]mess up dates again in the

future. To ^{9}make up for his ^{10}blunder, David ^{11}treated Jenny to a movie and afternoon tea in a fancy tea shop.

Total: 165 words

Vocabulary & Phrases in Use

1. **graduation** n. 畢業
2. **fall asleep** phr. 睡著
3. **take a shower** phr. 淋浴
4. **oversleep** v. 睡過頭
5. **apologize** v. 道歉
6. **promise** v. 保證

7. **stay up** phr. 熬夜
8. **mess up** phr. 搞砸
9. **make up for** phr. 彌補，補償
10. **blunder** n. 愚蠢的錯誤
11. **treat sb to sth**
　　用某物款待某人

Writing Tips

1. 寫作時須注意每一張圖片在時間上的變化，並運用時間副詞來銜接每一張圖片，且合理解釋故事的發展，例如：last Friday night 和 the next day。

2. 本文常見用法有 so...that... (如此…以至於…)，可在寫作時多加運用。

3. 本文結尾是男主角保證 (promise) 下次不會再犯了，並為了彌補他的過失 (To make up for his blunder) 而帶女主角去玩，可套用在類似情境的文章中。

3 Playing Tennis

請仔細觀察以下三幅連環圖片的內容，並想像第四幅圖片可能的
發展，然後寫出一篇涵蓋每張圖片內容且結局完整的故事。

Last Saturday morning, Julie called Matt. She wanted him to
teach her how to play tennis. Upon hearing this, Matt was so happy
because he had ^{1}admired Julie for a long time, and he wanted to
^{2}grab this chance to impress her! So, he happily agreed, and they
decided to meet each other on the ^{3}tennis court on Sunday. It was a
beautiful sunny day. They practiced for two hours until Julie felt it
was too hot to continue playing tennis.

^{4}In order to thank Matt for his help, Julie treated him to some
ice cream. When they were ^{5}enjoying themselves, Matt suddenly felt
a sharp pain in his ^{6}stomach. Seeing his face ^{7}twisted ^{8}in pain, Julie
called a taxi taking him to the hospital. Luckily, nothing was serious.
The doctor told Matt that he shouldn't have eaten ice cream so fast
^{9}on an empty stomach. However, this incident turned out to be ^{10}a

blessing in disguise: Matt became more familiar with Julie, thanks to the incident! Matt only admired Julie even more not just for her beauty but for her kindness.

Total: 182 words

Vocabulary & Phrases in Use

1. **admire** v. 仰慕
2. **grab** v. 抓住
3. **tennis court** n. 網球場
4. **in order to + V** phr. 為了…
5. **enjoy oneself** phr. 感到開心
6. **stomach** n. 胃
7. **twist** v. 扭曲
8. **in pain** 痛苦地
9. **on an empty stomach** phr. 空腹
10. **a blessing in disguise** n. 因禍得福

Writing Tips

1. 留意每一張圖片的流程，並運用想像力及對圖片的理解，清楚描述每一張圖片的情節變化，且注意描述每張圖片的篇幅盡量平均，以便連結並鋪陳故事的發展。

2. 本文常見用法有 too...to... (太…以至於不…)，例如：too hot to continue，以及 take sb to somewhere (帶某人到某處)，例如：take him to the hospital，還有表示與過去事實相反的假設語氣 (...shouldn't have eaten...)，可在寫作時多加運用。

3. 本文的故事內容前後呼應，男生本來想藉由教打球來令女生對自己印象深刻，沒想到卻因為空腹吃冰鬧肚子痛進了醫院，不過還好因禍得福讓他跟女生變更熟了。

4 Birthday Present

請仔細觀察以下三幅連環圖片的內容,並想像第四幅圖片可能的發展,然後寫出一篇涵蓋每張圖片內容且結局完整的故事。

One afternoon, Bill went to a ¹jewelry store to buy a birthday present for his girlfriend, Nancy. After a long and careful selection, Bill finally bought a beautiful ²necklace and had it gift-wrapped in a ³fancy box. As Bill was running late for the date with Nancy, he ran in a hurry. Suddenly, he ⁴bumped into a man carrying a ⁵similar box in hand ⁶rushing in his direction. The ⁷collision was so strong that they both dropped their boxes on the ground. After apologizing to each other, they picked up the boxes by their sides and left.

Later, when Bill saw Nancy, he proudly presented the box to her. Nancy opened the box ⁸only to see a ⁹necktie in it! She was upset and asked why Bill wanted to give her a necktie for her birthday. It suddenly dawned on Bill that he must have taken the wrong box after the hit. Thus, Bill explained what had happened earlier on the street. Nancy thought it was fun to have a necktie as a present [10]for a change. She then wore the necktie right away and went to her birthday celebration with Bill.

Total: 192 words

Vocabulary & Phrases in Use

1. **jewelry** n. 珠寶
2. **necklace** n. 項鍊
3. **fancy** adj. 精緻的
4. **bump** v. 撞
5. **similar** adj. 相似的
6. **rush** v. 飛奔
7. **collision** n. 相撞
8. **only to + V** 不料卻…
9. **necktie** n. 領帶
10. **for a change** phr. 做點改變

Writing Tips

1. 仔細觀察每一張圖片的線索之後再進行寫作，須清楚描述每一張圖片的內容，並給予合理的解釋，且注意描述每張圖片的篇幅盡量平均。

2. 本文常見用法有 only to + V (不料卻…)，以及 right away (立刻)，可在寫作時多加運用。

5 Typhoon

請仔細觀察以下三幅連環圖片的內容，並想像第四幅圖片可能的發展，然後寫出一篇涵蓋每張圖片內容且結局完整的故事。

Last Tuesday night, I stayed at home watching TV with my parents. According to the [1]weather forecast, a typhoon was [2]approaching fast. My dad told us that we should be well-prepared before it [3]made landfall. Therefore, he checked all the windows around the house first. [4]In addition, he got everything ready for the typhoon, such as a radio, a [5]flashlight, batteries, [6]instant noodles, and bottles of water. Because we were well-prepared, we didn't worry about the typhoon at all.

When the typhoon came, I could hear the wind [7]howling. Besides, heavy rain poured down. The typhoon was so [8]fierce that many trees were [9]rooted up. Suddenly, the power went off. Luckily, we had our flashlight and batteries ready. We listened to the radio and enjoyed instant noodles in the living room. The next morning, after the typhoon had passed, I found many [10]shop signs on the street damaged, and trash all over the place. It would take some time and effort for the city to [11]return to normal.

Total: 168 words

Vocabulary & Phrases in Use

1. **weather forecast** n. 天氣預報
2. **approach** v. 靠近
3. **make landfall** phr. (颱風) 登陸
4. **in addition** phr. 再者，而且
5. **flashlight** n. 手電筒
6. **instant noodles** n. 泡麵
7. **howl** v. (狂風) 呼嘯
8. **fierce** adj. 猛烈的
9. **root up** phr. 連根拔起
10. **shop sign** n. 商店招牌
11. **return to normal** 恢復原狀

Writing Tips

1. 本文以圖片連貫的主題「颱風」為主要的發展依據，運用轉折語描述每一張圖片的故事發展，以表達故事情節的變化，讓文章更具豐富性，例如：therefore、in addition、besides、suddenly。
2. 運用動詞和形容詞描述颱風來時的狀況，可讓文章更具生命力，例如：howl、pour down、fierce、root up。

6 Being Late for School

請仔細觀察以下三幅連環圖片的內容，並想像第四幅圖片可能的發展，然後寫出一篇涵蓋每張圖片內容且結局完整的故事。

It was June 16, Monday, 8 o'clock. [1]Even though the sun [2]shone brightly, Aaron was still [3]sound asleep. When he woke up, he realized that it was [4]definitely too late for school. Besides, it was the first day of the final exam. Thus, after changing his clothes quickly, he ran to the bus stop, only to see the bus leaving! He tried to catch the bus running behind it but soon realized that was a [5]mission impossible.

[6]By the time Aaron finally arrived at school, he was too late to take the test. He [7]dared not knock on the door and walk into the classroom while all his classmates were doing the test [8]attentively. As soon as the test was over, he asked his teacher for [9]forgiveness and a second chance to take the test. He told the teacher that he didn't go to bed until 4 a.m. that morning, so he failed to get up on

time. After scolding Aaron for his poor time [10]management, the teacher agreed to let him do the make-up test on one condition—he could not be late again in a week!

Total: 188 words

Vocabulary & Phrases in Use

1. **even though** phr. 即使
2. **shine** v. 照耀
3. **sound** adv. (睡得) 很沉地
4. **definitely** adv. 肯定地
5. **mission** n. 任務

6. **by the time...** phr. 當…時
7. **dare not + V** 不敢…
8. **attentively** adv. 專注地
9. **forgiveness** n. 原諒
10. **management** n. 管理

Writing Tips

1. 清楚描寫每一張圖片的內容 ， 並給予每一張圖片完整及合理的解釋，且注意描述每張圖片的篇幅盡量平均。

2. 本文從男主角呼呼大睡開頭，中間經歷突然驚醒、晚到學校、要求補考等波折，最後化險為夷，使文章更具趣味性。

3. 可多加運用副詞描述動詞或形容詞 ， 使文章更具多樣性，例如 ： brightly、definitely、quickly、finally、attentively。

4. 本文常見用法有 sb dare not + V (某人不敢…) 、 ask sb for forgiveness (請求某人原諒) ，以及 scold sb for sth (因為某事責備某人)，可套用在類似情境的文章中。

19

7 Taking Out the Garbage

請仔細觀察以下三幅連環圖片的內容，並想像第四幅圖片可能的發展，然後寫出一篇涵蓋每張圖片內容且結局完整的故事。

After cooking a fancy meal for her roommate, Emily found that her kitchen was [1]in a mess. [2]Pots and pans and all kinds of dishes were [3]scattered on the [4]kitchen counter. Besides putting everything back [5]in order, she needed to clean up the food waste, [6]recycle cans and bottles, and take out the garbage. Therefore, she tried to [7]sort the garbage in the kitchen according to [8]government [9]regulations. However, Emily was not familiar with this task, which thus took her quite a while.

When Emily was ready to take out the garbage, she heard the music from the garbage truck around the corner. She knew all her [10]neighbors were probably waiting there already. She was nervous because she knew the garbage truck would pass soon. Furthermore, she didn't want to keep the huge amount of garbage for one more day. So, she rushed down the stairs as fast as she could. Unfortunately, she fell down the stairs, and all the sorted garbage was scattered on the ground. Knowing that she couldn't throw her garbage away that evening, Emily had no choice but to put the garbage back in her house and had to bear the foul smell for one more day!

Total: 201 words

Vocabulary & Phrases in Use

1. **in a mess** phr. 亂七八糟
2. **pots and pans** n. 鍋碗瓢盆
3. **scatter** v. 散落
4. **kitchen counter** n. 廚房流理臺
5. **in order** phr. 按條理
6. **recycle** v. 回收
7. **sort** v. 分類
8. **government** n. 政府
9. **regulation** n. 規定
10. **neighbor** n. 鄰居

Writing Tips

1. 本文有 in a mess、scatter、recycle、sort、garbage truck 等用法，可在討論垃圾、環保、回收等類似情境的文章中多加運用。

2. 本文常見用法有 a fancy meal (一頓大餐) 以及分詞用法 (Knowing that..., Emily had no choice but to...)，可在寫作時多加運用。

3. 本文使用不同的轉折語表達時間或情境上的轉換，連貫描述每一張圖片的故事發展，讓文章更流暢，例如：besides、therefore、however、furthermore、so。

8 Making Noise

請仔細觀察以下三幅連環圖片的內容，並想像第四幅圖片可能的發展，然後寫出一篇涵蓋每張圖片內容且結局完整的故事。

After a long busy day, Kate decided to dine out with her two children. She went into a busy restaurant and ordered some dishes. However, there were not enough chairs, so Kate had to hold her ¹elder son, John, on her lap. When she tried to feed John, he started to ²cry out loud, for he wanted to have his own seat while dining. Hearing her brother crying, the baby girl, Jane, began crying out loud ³as well! Lying on the floor, John continued crying, grabbing at the ⁴tablecloth, and pulling it hard. Suddenly, the bowl of rice and one of the dishes on the table dropped onto the floor and broke into pieces. Such loud noise ⁵annoyed ⁶quite a few customers in the restaurant.

Therefore, the ⁷manager ⁸arranged a ⁹waiter to help out with the mess. The waiter explained to Kate that she needed to find a way to ^{10}calm her children down. Poor Kate explained that her boy needed a seat so he could eat properly. The waiter then decided to help her out by finding a chair for John and putting a teddy bear into Jane's arms. Finally, Kate could sit down and enjoy a quiet meal!

Total: 200 words

Vocabulary & Phrases in Use

1. **elder** adj. 較年長的
2. **cry out** phr. 大聲呼喊
3. **as well** phr. 也
4. **tablecloth** n. (餐桌的) 桌布
5. **annoy** v. 使惱怒
6. **quite a few** phr. 很多
7. **manager** n. 經理
8. **arrange** v. 安排
9. **waiter** n. 服務生
10. **calm...down** phr. 使…平靜下來

Writing Tips

1. 寫作時須密切注意圖片的情節變化，清楚描寫每一張圖片的內容，並給予每一張圖片合理的解釋，且注意描述每張圖片的篇幅盡量平均。

2. 當兩個句子的主詞相同時，可運用分詞來精簡句子，這用法可在寫作時多加運用，讓作文加分。例如本文有用到：Hearing her brother crying, the baby girl, Jane, began... 和 Lying on the floor, John continued...。

❾ A Horror Movie

請仔細觀察以下三幅連環圖片的內容，並想像第四幅圖片可能的
發展，然後寫出一篇涵蓋每張圖片內容且結局完整的故事。

Several weeks ago, Chris watched a [1]horror movie on TV. The
[2]leading role of the movie was a [3]scary ghost with an ugly face and
long hair. Chris felt [4]scared [5]throughout the film. After finishing
watching it, he turned off the TV and went to bed. He felt so
[6]frightened that he could not fall asleep until 11 p.m. Soon, he had a
[7]nightmare about the same ghost from the film coming to his
bedside.

Suddenly, with a [8]puff of cold wind, Chris awoke to find the
window [9]wide open. A strong feeling of horror [10]came over him as
he looked out the window. He saw a ghost with long hair covering
half the face standing near the window. He couldn't help [11]screaming
out loud. At the same time, his parents were [12]startled by his scream
and woke up from their sleep. They ran to his room right away and

found out that the person standing there was actually their neighbor, Maria, who [13]sleepwalks quite often. Finally, Chris' parents sent Maria home. Then, they gave Chris a hug and told him that everything was all right.

Total: 186 words

Vocabulary & Phrases in Use

1. **horror movie** n. 恐怖片
2. **leading role** n. 主角
3. **scary** adj. 嚇人的
4. **scared** adj. 害怕的
5. **throughout** prep. 自始至終
6. **frightened** adj. 驚嚇的
7. **nightmare** n. 惡夢
8. **puff** n. 一小縷 (空氣或風等)
9. **wide open** phr. 大開
10. **come over sb** phr. (感覺) 突然影響某人
11. **scream** v. 尖叫
12. **startle** v. 驚嚇
13. **sleepwalk** v. 夢遊

Writing Tips

1. 寫作時須仔細觀察圖片的情節變化，並清楚描寫每一張圖片的內容，舉本文為例：電視上和做夢夢到的人物是相同的、時鐘的時間等，並注意描述每張圖片的篇幅盡量平均。

2. 本文以圖片連貫的主題「恐怖片」為主要的發展依據，運用許多與驚嚇相關的字詞描繪人物和動作，例如：scary、scared、frightened、scream、startle，可在類似情境的文章中多加運用。

3. 本文常見用法有 come over sb (突然影響某人，讓某人突然感覺到)，可在寫作時多加運用。

❿ An Ideal Park (111 學測)

不同的公園，可能樣貌不同，特色也不同。請以此為主題，並依據下列兩張圖片的內容，寫一篇英文作文，文分兩段。第一段描述圖 A 和圖 B 中的公園各有何特色，第二段則說明你心目中理想公園的樣貌與特色，並解釋你的理由。

Since people have different ¹preferences for parks, there are ²various types of parks available nowadays. Depending on their aims, parks are equipped with different facilities. Take the two parks in the photos, for instance. Park A ³features open ground, ⁴slides, and gym equipment, all of which allow children to do outdoor activities, with their parents enjoying relaxing moments at the same time. Natural scenery ⁵are characteristic of Park B. With tall trees, a variety of plants, and a trim ⁶lawn, this park provides wonderful views for visitors to enjoy its beauty.

In my opinion, an ideal park should ⁷cater to the needs of citizens of all ages. Thus, there should first be equipment, such as slides and ⁸sandpits, for children to engage in health-promoting activities and to explore nature. Next, there should be gym equipment for adults, like exercise bikes, as an outlet for stress.

Lastly, large trees and plants planted along hiking [9]trails would be a bonus, providing [10]shades for the elderly to stroll in. In short, a well-designed park should be a green space that bonds citizens.

Total: 180 words

Vocabulary & Phrases in Use

1. **preference** n. 偏好，喜好
2. **various** adj. 各種不同的
3. **B feature A** B 的特色是 A
4. **slide** n. 滑梯
5. **A be characteristic of B**
   B 的特色是 A

6. **lawn** n. 草地，草坪
7. **cater to** phr. 滿足，迎合
8. **sandpit** n. 沙坑
9. **trail** n. 小路，小徑
10. **shade** n. 陰涼處

Writing Tips

1. 在圖片寫作中，務必先留意題目要求並看清楚圖片細節。第一段可從公園的功能下筆，務必將圖 A 和圖 B 中公園各自的特色具體描寫出來。第二段要具體說明心目中理想公園的樣貌與特色，並解釋理由。兩段都是描述事實，用現在式。

2. 本文常見用法有第一段的 B feature A (B 的特色是 A)、數量詞 + of which (all of which)、with + O + OC (with their parents enjoying)、A be characteristic of B (B 的特色是 A)；第二段則有複合形容詞 N-V-ing (health-promoting)，以及 V_1, V_2-ing (be a bonus, providing shades)，並用 first、next、lastly 來列點舉例。

⑪ Water Shortage (110 學測試辦)

你認為下面兩張圖片中呈現的是什麼景象?你對這些景象有什麼感想?請根據圖片內容,寫一篇英文作文,文分兩段。第一段描述兩張圖片的內容,包括其中的人、事、物以及發生的事情;第二段討論導致這個現象可能的原因,並說明你認為未來可以採取什麼具體的因應措施,以避免類似景象再度發生。

Living in Taiwan, I never thought about water [1]shortage problems. It shocked people that no typhoons made landfall last year. Nevertheless, most people still continued their original habits of using water, the consequence of which was that major [2]reservoirs [3]were running low. Take Sun Moon Lake, for example. With the water levels dropping, the bottom of the lake [4]dried up and the land [5]cracked open. Many people's lives were affected for lack of water. Owing to the enforcement of water [6]rationing, people had no option but to get water from water trucks for their daily use. It was then that I realized how terrible water shortage was.

This is the worst [7]drought in a decade. I suppose the reasons are as follows. The first one is [8]global warming, which is blamed for the reduced number of typhoons hitting Taiwan. Much of the water in Taiwan comes from the rain brought along by typhoons. Fewer typhoons mean less rain. The second reason is people's [9]wasteful habits of using water. To prevent this crisis from [10]escalating, people can effectively reduce the amount of water used by taking shorter showers and using recycled water. In conclusion, we must change our habits in case water shortage occurs again in the future.

Total: 207 words

Vocabulary & Phrases in Use

1. **shortage** n. 缺乏，缺少
2. **reservoir** n. 水庫
3. **be running low** phr. 快沒了
4. **dry up** phr. 乾涸
5. **crack** v. 裂開
6. **rationing** n. 配給
7. **drought** n. 旱災
8. **global warming** n. 全球暖化
9. **wasteful** adj. 浪費的
10. **escalate** v. 加劇，惡化

Writing Tips

1. 在圖片寫作中，務必先留意題目要求並看清楚圖片細節。第一段描述兩張圖片的內容與感想，敘述已經發生的故事用過去式。第二段分析導致此現象的原因，並必須提出具體的因應措施才能得高分。

2. 本文常見用法有轉折語 nevertheless，以及第一段用 which 代替前述句子 (the consequence of which)、分裂句 it was...that...，還有第二段的 N + pp (water used...)、in case。

⓬ Going to an Anniversary Sale (109 學測)

請觀察以下有關某家賣場週年慶的新聞報導圖片，並根據圖片內容想像其中發生的一個事件或故事，寫一篇英文作文，文長約 120 個單詞。文分兩段，第一段描述兩張圖片中所呈現的場景，以及正在發生的狀況或事件；第二段則敘述該事件 (或故事) 接下來的發展和結果。

　　Amy went to a department store anniversary sale with her mom, who ¹set her heart on a ²brand-name bag limited in number. In order to successfully get their hands on the bag, they hurried to the department store in the early morning. However, to their surprise, there had been a long line. As soon as the door opened, what people did was push each other, ³elbowing their way to their desired products. Fearing injury might happen in such ⁴chaos, Amy's mom had to pull her away from the crowd.

　　Nevertheless, the story didn't end here. To get real ⁵bargains, Amy's mom still ⁶resolved to reach the bag shop, but she told Amy to wait for her in a quieter place for Amy's safety. Amy's mom almost ⁷lost her footing as she struggled to get the bag! After they finished shopping, Amy ⁸breathed a sigh of relief. This was the worst shopping experience she'd ever had. What's worse, her mom found that the bag was stained, which she had not noticed in such [9]haste. Therefore, they decided to ask for a [10]refund, which means they must return to the "[11]battlefield." Misfortunes seem to never come singly...

Total: 195 words

Vocabulary & Phrases in Use

1. **set one's heart on sth** phr.
   非常想要…，一心想要…
2. **brand-name** adj. 知名品牌的
3. **elbow one's way to...** phr.
   用手肘開路朝…擠過去
4. **chaos** n. 混亂
5. **bargain** n. 便宜貨
6. **resolve** v. 決定，下決心
7. **lose one's footing** phr. 沒站穩
8. **breathe a sigh of relief** phr.
   鬆了一口氣
9. **haste** n. 倉促匆忙
10. **refund** n. 退款
11. **battlefield** n. 戰場

Writing Tips

1. 在圖片寫作中，務必先留意題目要求並看清楚圖片細節，依照題目的提示寫作。第一段描述兩張圖片的內容，以及正在發生的故事。第二段敘述故事的發展。敘述已經發生的故事用過去式。

2. 本文常見用法有第一段的 what + S + V + is/was + V (what people did was push...) 與 V₁, V₂-ing (push..., elbowing...)，以及第二段用 which 代替前述句子 (the bag was stained, which she had not noticed)。

⑬ Favorite Types of News (108 指考)

右表顯示美國 18 至 29 歲的青
年對不同類別之新聞的關注度
統計。請依據圖表內容寫一篇
英文作文，文長至少 120 個單
詞。文分二段，第一段描述圖
表內容，並指出關注度較高及
偏低的類別；第二段則描述在
這六個新聞類別中，你自己較
為關注及較不關注的新聞主題
分別為何，並說明理由。

美國青年關注之新聞類別

環境與天然災害 ▮69%
社會議題 ▮64%
國際事務 ▮59%
娛樂與名人 ▮58%
學校與教育 ▮49%
藝術與文化 ▮30%

■ 數字顯示關注度之百分比

This bar chart clearly ¹illustrates the six types of news that
American teenagers pay attention to. As can be seen, news stories
about environmental and natural ²disasters as well as social ³issues
have attracted most American teenagers' attention, with the
⁴percentage being 69% and 64% respectively. In contrast, news
about art and culture seems to draw the least attention from them,
which ⁵accounts for only 30%.

I myself am mostly concerned about environmental and natural
disasters. ⁶Plenty of research has ⁷indicated that pollution and
natural disasters have profoundly impacted our lives, with the former
⁸deteriorating our living conditions and health, and the latter
claiming numerous lives. Moreover, activities damaging the
environment can contribute to natural disasters. For example,
deforestation can cause mudslides. As a result, it is our duty to care

about how to stop people from harming our environment. However, what appeals to me the least is the news about entertainment and [9]celebrities. As a high school student, I need to acquire knowledge and broaden my horizons with the goal of entering a [10]distinguished college and finding an ideal job. [11]Hence, it is important that I catch up on current big events or anything that can help me gain wisdom rather than news stories about individual celebrities, which mainly serve as [12]day-to-day gossip topics.

Total: 215 words

Vocabulary & Phrases in Use

1. **illustrate** v. (以圖表等) 說明
2. **disaster** n. 災害，災難
3. **issue** n. 議題
4. **percentage** n. 百分比，百分率
5. **account for** phr. 占…數量
6. **plenty** pron. 許多，大量

7. **indicate** v. 顯示
8. **deteriorate** v. (使) 惡化
9. **celebrity** n. 名人
10. **distinguished** adj. 傑出的
11. **hence** adv. 因此
12. **day-to-day** adj. 日常的

Writing Tips

1. 進行圖表寫作時，務必先留意題目、看清楚圖表所要表達的涵義。第一段必須先看懂圖表，依照題目要求，描述最高與最低的類別，並加以分析。第二段具體描述自己的情形並說明理由。兩段都是描述事實，時態使用現在式。

2. 本文常見用法有第一段用來表達比較的 in contrast，以及第二段在延伸說明應該做到的事情並說明完原因後，最後用來作總結的 Hence, it is important that...。

33

⒕ A Blessing in Disguise (106 學測)

請仔細觀察以下三幅連環圖片的內容，並想像第四幅圖片可能的
發展，然後寫出一篇涵蓋每張圖片內容且結局完整的故事。

It was a beautiful Sunday with the sun shining brightly in the sky. Jason decided to take a trip with his family. His wife, Helen, and his daughter, Amy, were all ¹thrilled about it. ²Humming his favorite song and putting baggage into the ³trunk, Jason was ⁴delighted to see the smiles on their faces. However, the smiles soon turned into ⁵long faces when they were ⁶stuck in a heavy traffic jam, which forced them to move ⁷at a snail's pace on the ⁸highway.

After two hours, they ⁹eventually arrived at their ¹⁰destination! When they reached the gate, the huge crowd again ¹¹threw cold water on their plan. Having been out for several hours and still getting nowhere, they decided to go home instead of waiting in line. On their way home, Jason ¹²accidentally took a wrong turn, and they found a big park they had never seen before, and there were no lines!

It was such a nice place for a picnic. In the end, they had a wonderful picnic in the sun in the pretty park! Things not going as planned turned out to be a blessing in disguise!

Total: 190 words

Vocabulary & Phrases in Use

1. **thrilled** adj. 極為興奮的
2. **hum** v. 哼歌
3. **trunk** n. 後車箱
4. **delighted** adj. 令人愉快的
5. **long face** n. 沮喪的臉
6. **stuck** adj. 動不了的
7. **at a snail's pace** phr. 緩慢地

8. **highway** n. 公路
9. **eventually** adv. 終於
10. **destination** n. 目的地
11. **throw cold water on sth** phr. 對…潑冷水
12. **accidentally** adv. 意外地

Writing Tips

1. 寫作時須仔細觀察圖片的情節變化，清楚描寫每一張圖片內容，並注意描述每張圖片的篇幅盡量平均。
2. 本文使用 shine brightly (明亮地照耀)，與第 6 篇 "Being Late for School" 文章用法相同，可在形容陽光耀眼時多加運用。
3. 本文常見用法有同位語 (His wife, Helen, and his daughter, Amy, were...)、分詞用法 (Humming his favorite song..., Jason was delighted...) 以及被動式 (were stuck in a heavy traffic jam)，可在寫作時多加運用。

⑮ Road Safety (103 學測)

請仔細觀察以下三幅連環圖片的內容，並想像第四幅圖片可能的發展，寫一篇涵蓋所有連環圖片內容且有完整結局的故事。

Last Thursday afternoon, Amy and her brother, Ted, left school together for home. As usual, they were using [1]smartphones while walking along the road. Amy and Ted [2]were so absorbed in using their phones that they failed to notice what lay in front of them. Just when Amy was staring at the screen of her phone, she bumped into a tree. Feeling [3]dizzy right away, she dropped the phone on the ground. Right behind her was a mother with her child. Seeing what had happened, the mother was surprised and reminded her child never to use the phone while walking.

[4]Meanwhile, Ted was listening to his music at a high [5]volume while walking. He [6]was not aware of a car approaching from behind. Seeing the student right in front of his car, the driver was so mad that he furiously [7]honked the horn while slamming on the [8]brakes.

One of the ⁹passers-by rushed to ¹⁰pat Ted on the shoulder and pulled him away from the road. Ted finally took off his headphones and heard his sister ¹¹crying over her bleeding forehead and the broken phone.

Total: 185 words

Vocabulary & Phrases in Use

1. **smartphone** n. 智慧型手機
2. **be absorbed in...** 專注於…
3. **dizzy** adj. 暈眩的
4. **meanwhile** adv. 同時
5. **volume** n. 音量
6. **be aware of...** 察覺到…

7. **honk the horn** 按汽車喇叭
8. **brake** n. 剎車
9. **passer-by** n. 路人
10. **pat sb on sth** 輕拍某人某部位
11. **cry over...** 為…哭泣

Writing Tips

1. 本文以 Last Thursday afternoon... 為開頭，動詞時態宜用過去式，並按照時間先後順序清楚描述每一張圖片的情節變化，且注意描述每張圖片的篇幅盡量平均。

2. 本文常見用法有 bump into sth (撞上某物) 和 right away (馬上)，並有以 while (當…) 所引導的時間副詞子句 (...while walking along the road.)。在 while 之後通常接進行式表示同時進行或持續的動作。

3. 寫作時可適時運用片語和副詞，讓故事的起承轉合更為順暢，例如：as usual、meanwhile、finally。

16 Time Management (103 指考)

下圖呈現的是美國某高中的全體學生每天進行各種活動的時間
分配，請寫一篇至少 120 個單詞的英文作文。文分兩段，第一段
描述該圖所呈現之特別現象；第二段請說明整體而言，你一天的
時間分配與該高中全體學生的異同，並說明其理由。

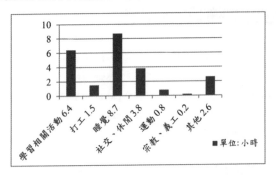

The [1]bar chart shows how the high school students in the U.S.
manage their time. [2]To begin with, studying doesn't take up most of
their lives. They only spend around one-fourth of a day doing
[3]academic activities. Besides, they get enough sleep and [4]hang out
with friends or do exercise. What surprises me the most is that they
even have extra time to do [5]part-time or [6]voluntary work.

[7]In contrast with their daily schedule, mine is [8]completely
[9]dominated by studying. I spend more than eight hours a day at
school. I don't have time to pursue my hobbies or to hang out with
friends. [10]Worst of all, I consider sleeping a [11]luxury because lots of
homework [12]deprives me of sleep. I wish someday I could manage

my own time like the high school students in the U.S. instead of
[13]being burdened with studying.

Total: 143 words

Vocabulary & Phrases in Use

1. **bar chart** n. 長條圖
2. **to begin with** phr. 首先
3. **academic** adj. 學業的
4. **hang out with sb** phr.
   與某人閒晃
5. **part-time** adj. 兼職的
6. **voluntary work** n. 志工工作
7. **in contrast with...** phr.
   與⋯對比

8. **completely** adv. 完全地
9. **dominate** v. 支配
10. **worst of all** phr. 最糟糕的是
11. **luxury** n. 奢侈 (品)
12. **deprive sb of...** 剝奪某人的⋯
13. **be burdened with...** phr.
    負擔⋯

Writing Tips

1. 進行看圖表寫作時，務必先看清楚圖表所要表達的涵義。第一段先說明此長條圖所代表的意義，並加以分析，同時找出值得特別說明的「亮點」，時態用現在式。第二段點出自己在時間分配上與美國高中生相同或不同之處，加以比較並說明理由。

2. 本文常見用法有 to begin with (首先)、in contrast with... (與⋯對比)、worst of all (最糟糕的是)，以及運用動名詞當作句子的主詞 (studying doesn't take up...)，還有適時運用被動式 (being burdened with...)，可在寫作時多加運用，讓文章更加活潑。

39

17 A Lesson in Selfishness (102 學測)

請仔細觀察以下三幅連環圖片的內容，並想像第四幅圖片可能的
發展，寫出一個涵蓋連環圖片內容並有完整結局的故事。

Last Wednesday was an ¹exhausting day. After the midterm
exam, I took the MRT home. I was lucky enough to spot a ²vacant
seat, not noticing that it was a ³priority seat. Though I could see an
old man standing in front of me, I was too tired to ⁴yield my seat to
him. Several days later, while I was playing basketball, I fell and
⁵sprained my right ⁶ankle. It hurt so bad that I could hardly get up.
With my classmate's help, I went to see a doctor and learned that I
had to walk with a ⁷crutch for a few weeks.

The next day, to my ⁸disappointment, nobody gave up his or
her seat to me on the MRT. The girl sitting on the priority seat
⁹ignored me ¹⁰intentionally just as what I had done to the elderly
man. When I stood there painfully, I remembered what Confucius
said, "Don't do to others what you would not have them do to you."

I ¹¹was ashamed of my ¹²previous selfish behavior, and I vowed that I would never be that selfish again.

Total: 184 words

Vocabulary & Phrases in Use

1. **exhausting** adj. 累人的
2. **vacant** adj. 空的
3. **priority seat** n. 博愛座
4. **yield sth to sb** 讓某物給某人
5. **sprain** v. 扭傷
6. **ankle** n. 腳踝
7. **crutch** n. 拐杖

8. **disappointment** n. 失望
9. **ignore** v. 忽視
10. **intentionally** adv. 故意地
11. **be ashamed of...**
    對…感到羞愧的
12. **previous** adj. 先前的

Writing Tips

1. 本文常見用法有 with one's help (藉助某人的幫助) 和 to one's disappointment (令某人失望的是…)，以及分詞用法 (I was..., not noticing...)，可在寫作時多加運用。

2. 本文以圖片連貫的主題「讓座」為主要的發展依據，運用 vacant、priority seat、yield sth to sb 等用法來寫作，可套用在類似情境的文章中。

3. 本文最後引用孔子語錄「己所不欲，勿施於人」(Don't do to others what you would have them do to you.)，可在類似情境的文章中多加運用。

18 Love at First Sight (100 學測)

請仔細觀察以下三幅連環圖片的內容，並想像第四幅圖片可能的
發展，寫出一個涵蓋連環圖片內容並有完整結局的故事。

One night, Harry went to a ^{1}costume party. As a ^{2}clumsy
dancer, he ^{3}could do nothing but stand alone in the corner.
Suddenly, an ^{4}elegant girl wearing a crown and a beautiful dress
^{5}caught his eye. It was ^{6}love at first sight! However, he couldn't
find a chance to talk to the girl. Luckily, his friend helped him get
the girl's address.

Harry decided to bring his guitar and sang to the girl outside her
home, hoping to ^{7}impress her with his love songs. Therefore, the
next day, he sang ^{8}in the moonlight for hours, passionately gazing at
the window of the girl's home. Nevertheless, instead of the
^{9}charming girl, a man with curly hair ^{10}showed up in the window and
yelled at Harry to ^{11}shut up! Harry was shocked and asked the man if
he knew the girl who went to the costume party last night. The man

started to laugh loudly and hollered, "The girl with a crown and a dress? That was ME! Don't forget that it was a costume party!" Harry felt so embarrassed that he ran back home right away.

Total: 185 words

Vocabulary & Phrases in Use

1. **costume party** n. 化妝舞會
2. **clumsy** adj. 笨拙的
3. **can do nothing but V** 不得不…
4. **elegant** adj. 優雅的
5. **catch one's eye** phr. 引起某人注意
6. **love at first sight** phr. 一見鍾情
7. **impress sb with sth** 使某人對某事印象深刻
8. **in the moonlight** 月光下
9. **charming** adj. 迷人的
10. **show up** phr. 出現
11. **shut up** 閉嘴

Writing Tips

1. 本文以 One night 為開頭，動詞時態宜用過去式，並按照時間先後順序描述。故事需完整且有創意，舉本文為例，主角在化妝舞會上將一名男子誤認為優雅的女子。

2. 本文常見用法有 can do nothing but V (不得不…)、分詞用法 (Harry decided..., hoping... 以及 ...he sang..., passionately gazing...)，可在寫作時多加運用，使文章更加豐富。

3. 有些轉折語有近義詞，例如：however、nevertheless，可在寫作時交替使用，並注意各轉折語的使用方式和在句子裡擺放的位置。

⑲ Honesty Is the Best Policy (99 學測)

請仔細觀察以下三幅連環圖片的內容，並想像第四幅圖片可能的發展，寫出一個涵蓋連環圖片內容並有完整結局的故事。

    Mrs. Liao ran a noodle shop near Hsinchu Railway Station with her only son, A-Ming. A-Ming usually helped his mom with some chores after school. One day, a man came and ordered a bowl of beef noodles. He ¹devoured the noodles ²in no time and left in a hurry. As soon as he left, A-Ming found a ³leather bag on the ⁴stool. ⁵Out of curiosity, he and his mom opened the bag carefully. ⁶To their great surprise, they found ⁷piles of thousand-dollar bills inside!

    ⁸At the same time, in the station the man found his bag had ⁹disappeared. Nevertheless, he could hardly think of any place where he might have lost it. He asked the ticket office staff there, but his bag had not yet been sent to the lost-and-found. Feeling worried, he rushed to the police station to report his bag missing. Just when he was describing the leather bag to the police officer, A-Ming and

his mom walked into the police station with the bag. The man was so happy to find his bag. He thanked A-Ming and his mom many times. To show his gratitude, he [10]rewarded them with one hundred thousand dollars in the end.

Total: 199 words

Vocabulary & Phrases in Use

1. **devour** v. 狼吞虎嚥
2. **in no time** phr. 馬上
3. **leather** n. 皮革
4. **stool** n. 凳子
5. **out of curiosity** 出於好奇心
6. **to one's surprise**
   令某人驚訝地
7. **piles of...** 一大堆⋯
8. **at the same time** phr. 同時
9. **disappear** v. 消失不見
10. **reward sb with sth**
    以某物酬謝某人

Writing Tips

1. 本篇看圖寫作為記敘文，動詞時態宜用過去式，須清楚地描述每一張圖片的故事情節，並注意描述每張圖片的篇幅盡量平均。
2. 寫作時，記得適時運用連接詞、轉折語和分詞用法 (Feeling worried, he rushed to...)，可使文章更為通順有趣。
3. 本文常見用法有 in no time (馬上)、in a hurry (匆忙)、hardly (幾乎不) 和 show one's gratitude (表達某人的感謝之意)，可在寫作時多加運用。

⑳ A Collapsed Building (98 學測)

請根據右方圖片的場景，描述整個事
件發生的前因後果。文章請分兩段，
第一段說明**之前**發生了什麼事情，並
根據圖片內容描述**現在**的狀況；第二
段請合理說明**接下來**可能會發生什麼
事，或者**未來**該做些什麼。

Last night, a fierce typhoon ¹struck Nantou with high winds
and heavy rain. Many trees were ²uprooted, and quite a few ³utility
poles fell in the middle of the road as well. Some houses nearby
were also damaged. The Wang family's house was one of them. The
whole family was forced to ⁴evacuate from their home without
having time to grab anything with them. ⁵Furniture and ⁶valuable
items in the house were also ⁷destroyed.

Since they have lost almost everything due to this typhoon, they
worry what may happen to their lives in the future. The government
places them in the ⁸temporary ⁹shelter and gives them some money
to meet their ¹⁰urgent needs. The rest of the community members
also lend their helping hands by donating money and basic
¹¹necessities to the Wang family. Seeing how everyone around them
is trying their best to help them out, the Wang family believes that
their life will be back to normal in no time.

Total: 162 words

1. **strike** v. 侵襲
2. **uproot** v. 連根拔起
3. **utility pole** n. 電線桿
4. **evacuate** v. 撤離
5. **furniture** n. 家具
6. **valuable** adj. 貴重的

7. **destroy** v. 破壞
8. **temporary** adj. 暫時的
9. **shelter** n. 避難所
10. **urgent** adj. 緊急的
11. **necessity** n. 必需品

Writing Tips

1. 圖片顯示為一棟倒塌的房舍，寫作前先設想好發生什麼事以及前因後果，可以是颱風後的場景，或是地震後的災區現場，也可以是戰爭後的情景。

2. 本文與第 5 篇 "Typhoon" 文章的主題「颱風」相同，運用生動的動詞 (uproot、damage、destroy) 和形容詞 (fierce、heavy) 描述颱風來襲的狀況以及帶來的災害。

3. 寫作時須注意常見名詞的搭配詞用法，例如：high winds 及 heavy rain。

4. 本文有分詞用法 (Seeing..., the Wang family believes...)，並適時運用時間副詞，例如：last night 及 in no time，讓文章更加流暢。

5. 本文常見用法有 shelter (避難所)，與第 81 篇 "Campus Safety" 文章用法相同，可在類似情境的文章中多加運用。

21 A Letter to...

請寫一封信給某人，可以是你的親友，也可以是你不認識的人，如偶像歌手、知名作家，甚至是歷史人物，寫下你想對他或她說的話。

請注意：請以 Alan 或 Alice 在信末署名，**不得使用自己的真實中文或英文名字**。

Dear sister,

    I would like to thank you for your help. Without your ¹encouragement, I would not have ²succeeded in passing the ³entrance exams. Last year, I couldn't stop reading a series of ⁴comic books. Even if my entrance exams were ⁵around the corner, I still ⁶couldn't help but do it. Mom and Dad saw me ⁷neglect my studies, so they scolded me for wasting my time on comic books. However, I refused to listen to them.

    Fortunately, it was you, my lovely sister, who never ⁸gave up on me. You were kind, ⁹patient, and ¹⁰considerate. You talked to me, encouraged me, and listened to me. After many long conversations with you, I finally found that Mom, Dad, and you were so worried about me. At that moment, I felt very ¹¹regretful. ¹²From then on, I ¹³made up my mind to stop reading comic books and to start preparing for the exams. I'm extremely ¹⁴grateful to you for your love and encouragement. Thank you so much!

Love,

Alice

Total: 168 words

1. **encouragement** n. 鼓勵

2. **succeed in...** 順利完成⋯

3. **entrance exam** n. 入學考試

4. **comic book** n. 漫畫書

5. **around the corner** phr.
   即將來臨

6. **can't help but + V**
   不禁⋯，忍不住⋯

7. **neglect one's studies**
   忽略某人的學業

8. **give up on...** phr. 放棄⋯

9. **patient** adj. 耐心的

10. **considerate** adj. 體貼的

11. **regretful** adj. 後悔的

12. **from then on** phr. 從那時起

13. **make up one's mind to...**
    phr. 某人下定決心做⋯

14. **grateful** adj. 感激的

Writing Tips

1. 書信的格式通常包含「稱呼語」、「內文」、「結尾語」和「署名」。
   「結尾語」因寫信的對象不同，使用上有所差異：用於親人可用
   Love；用於長輩可用 Respectfully；用於平輩可用 Sincerely 或
   Best regards。須注意結尾語中的第一個字首要大寫，且在末尾要有
   一個逗點。

2. 本文常見用法有 around the corner (即將來臨)、can't help but + V
   (不禁⋯) 和 make up one's mind to... (某人下定決心做⋯)，以及假
   設語氣 Without..., I would not have... (若沒有⋯我就沒辦法⋯)，可
   套用在類似情境的文章中。

22 An Apology Letter to My Parents

請以書信格式敘述你曾經犯過的一個錯誤，並詳述其原因。同時告訴你的父母你要如何彌補這個過錯。信件開頭為 Dear Mom and Dad, I'm sorry that I... 。

請注意：請以 William 或 Wendy 在信末署名，**不得使用自己的真實中文或英文名字**。

Dear Mom and Dad,

I'm sorry that I have to [1]admit to you that I made a mistake last night. Yesterday was your 20th wedding [2]anniversary, and we had a fancy dinner celebration together. After dinner, Dad showed us a [3]precious wedding [4]album. It was my first time to see the wedding photos of yours. I was so excited to [5]look over them by myself in my room again. However, I spilled black tea on the photo album accidentally. One of the photos was [6]stained. At that time, I was so nervous and tried to [7]wipe it clean. I knew these photos were very important to you.

Therefore, I [8]came up with an idea to [9]make it up to you. In order to better preserve the photos, I would [10]scan all of them and store them well on the computer. Now, I'm writing you this letter asking for your forgiveness. I promise you that I will be careful with those photos when I scan them into the computer. I hope you can forgive me for my carelessness.

Lots of love,

William

Total: 181 words

Vocabulary & Phrases in Use

1. **admit** v. 承認
2. **anniversary** n. 週年紀念日
3. **precious** adj. 珍貴的
4. **album** n. 相冊
5. **look over** phr. 查看
6. **stain** v. 弄髒，沾到汙漬

7. **wipe** v. 擦拭
8. **come up with** phr. 想出
9. **make it up to sb** phr.
   補償某人
10. **scan** v. 掃描

Writing Tips

1. 本文以 I'm sorry that I... 為開頭，可看出是一封道歉信，根據提示，信中必須呈現的主要內容為敘述自己的錯誤和原因，以及要如何彌補過錯。結尾以請求原諒 (I'm writing you this letter asking for your forgiveness.) 作結。

2. 注意簡函寫作的基本格式，須具備「稱呼語」、「內文」、「結尾語」和「署名」，「內文」包括問候語、內容、結尾，本文是寫給父母親，結尾語可用 Love 或 Lots of love 等。

3. 本文常見用法有 It was my first time to... (這是我第一次…)、come up with (想出) 和 make it up to sb (補償某人)，可套用在類似情境的文章中。

23 A Letter to a Friend

請你 (英文名字必須假設為 Ray 或 Jennifer) 寫一封信，信件對象則是一位好友 (英文名字必須假設為 Jeffrey 或 Tiffany)。第一段描述你的近況，第二段寫未來的計畫。

請注意：必須使用上述的 Ray 或 Jennifer 在信末署名，**不得使用自己的真實中文或英文名字**。

Dear Jeffrey,

How have you been recently? It has been quite a long time since we last saw each other. I hope everything is fine with you and your family. I've been ¹occupied with my ²schoolwork because the entrance exam is around the corner. Besides, the graduation ³ceremony is ⁴under way, so I've been busy all the time. However, I'm ⁵content with my student life. I always have a lot of things to do, and thus I find time passes quickly.

After the entrance exam, I plan to go abroad for a summer travel study program in London. London is the city where I want to go the most around the world. Since I'm so ⁶enthusiastic about English ⁷literature, and I also need to ⁸sharpen my English skills, London as a historic city definitely serves my needs. The plan for a two-month trip to London seems to be a good idea, doesn't it?

What is your plan for your summer vacation? I hope to ⁹hear from you and see you soon.

¹⁰Sincerely,

Jennifer

Total: 173 words

Vocabulary & Phrases in Use

1. **occupied** adj. 忙碌的

2. **schoolwork** n. 學校作業

3. **ceremony** n. 典禮

4. **under way** phr. 進行中

5. **content** adj. 滿意的

6. **enthusiastic** adj. 熱情的

7. **literature** n. 文學

8. **sharpen** v. 加強

9. **hear from sb** phr. 收到某人的音訊

10. **Sincerely (yours),** phr. 敬上，謹上 (用作書信結尾語)

Writing Tips

1. 本文開頭 How have you been recently? (你近來過得如何呢？) 為典型的問候語，可套用在許多書信的開頭。

2. 本文的第二段內容 I plan to go abroad... 可套用在描述旅遊計畫、最想去的城市或國家等類似情境的文章中。

3. 本文的結論語句是 I hope to hear from you..., 用來表達期待對方的回覆，類似的用法還有 I look forward to your reply., 可套用在類似情境的書信中。

24 A Birthday Party Invitation Letter

你的生日快到了，你想邀請你的好朋友一起來慶祝。你 (英文名字必須假設為 Billy 或 Ann) 打算寫一封信給他 / 她 (英文名字必須假設為 Joe 或 Jane)，第一段請邀請你的朋友，附上時間與地點等資料；第二段請說明你打算如何和朋友一起慶祝你的生日。請注意：必須使用上述的 Billy 或 Ann 在信末署名，**不得使用自己的真實中文或英文名字**。

Dear Jane,

My birthday is ¹coming up soon, and I would like to invite you to my birthday party. I'll turn 18 this July, and I can't think of a better way to celebrate it than spend time with my best friends and classmates. I'll throw a party in my house on Saturday, July 9th at 2 p.m. Please let me know if you are ²available that day!

The party will ³include some ⁴activities and a big dinner prepared by me and my family. When you guys arrive in the afternoon, we can play some ⁵board games. My parents love board games, and we have a ⁶collection of them. Then, we can take a walk ⁷at sunset along the river. This may sound like a boring thing to do for you. But you know what? The river is lined with beautiful silver grass, swaying with golden sparkles under the setting sun. A sight that will leave you speechless and linger in your mind! Finally, we will enjoy dinner and a ⁸homemade cake together. How does that sound to you? I ⁹look forward to hearing from you soon.

¹⁰Kind regards,

Billy

Total: 197 words

Vocabulary & Phrases in Use

1. **come up** phr. 即將到來
2. **available** adj. 有空的
3. **include** v. 包含
4. **activity** n. 活動
5. **board game** n. 桌上遊戲
6. **collection** n. 收藏
7. **at sunset** 在傍晚日落時
8. **homemade** adj. 手工的
9. **look forward to** phr. 盼望
10. **Kind regards,** phr. 致上親切的問候，敬上，謹上 (用作書信結尾語)

Writing Tips

1. 本文是寫給好朋友，結尾語可用 Kind regards、Warm regards 或 Warm wishes 等。

2. 本文的開頭 I would like to invite you to my... 為典型的邀約用語，可套用在類似的邀請信件中。

3. 本文的結論語句是 I look forward to hearing from you... 用來表達期待對方的回覆，可套用在類似情境的書信中。

4. 本文提及的派對計畫可套用在類似情境的書信或文章中，用來說明如何規劃活動、建議活動的內容或是敘述參加過最有趣或最無聊的聚會等。

55

25 A Declining Letter

你的朋友邀請你參加他／她的生日派對，而你不想或不能參加。你 (英文名字必須假設為 Joe 或 Jane) 打算寫一封信給他／她 (英文名字必須假設為 Billy 或 Ann)，委婉回絕他／她的邀請，並說明拒絕的原因。

請注意：必須使用上述的 Joe 或 Jane 在信末署名，**不得使用自己的真實中文或英文名字**。

Dear Billy,

Thank you so much for inviting me to your 18th birthday party. I've just received your [1]invitation card. I'd like to go, but I'm afraid that I won't be able to go to your party because of a [2]prior [3]engagement.

My brother who lives in Canada will arrive on the night of your birthday party. I haven't seen him for quite a long time, and I miss him so much. My parents and I are going to [4]pick him up at the airport, and we will go to a [5]local restaurant for dinner together. So, it's a [6]pity that I won't be able to attend your birthday party. I'm very sorry about that.

I'm sending you all my best wishes and may every wish you make [7]come true! Happy birthday to you! May God [8]bless you with good health, happiness, and [9]success!

[10]Warmest regards,

Jane

Total: 144 words

Vocabulary & Phrases in Use

1. **invitation** n. 邀請
2. **prior** adj. 之前的
3. **engagement** n. 約會
4. **pick sb up** phr. 開車接某人
5. **local** adj. 當地的
6. **pity** n. 可惜
7. **come true** phr. 實現
8. **bless** v. 祝福
9. **success** n. 成功
10. **Warmest regards,** phr. 致上最溫暖的問候，敬上，謹上（用作書信結尾語）

Writing Tips

1. 本文也是寫給好朋友，結尾語同樣可用 Warmest regards、Kind regards 或 Best wishes 等。

2. 本文的結論語句是 May God bless you with...，用來表達祝福對方，常用作書信結尾的祝福語，可套用在類似情境的書信中。

3. 本文開頭先說明感激之意，再說明無法參加的原因，其中所用之 prior engagement 是相當好用且不傷感情的婉拒用語，可套用在婉拒邀約等類似情境的書信或是對話中。

26 A Congratulation Letter

你的堂／表兄姊準備要結婚，你 (英文名字必須假設為 Dave 或 Jill) 打算寫一封信恭賀他／她 (英文名字必須假設為 Tom 或 Abbie)。

請注意：必須使用上述的 Dave 或 Jill 在信末署名，**不得使用自己的真實中文或英文名字**。

Dear Abbie,

How have you been? I'm so happy to hear that you are getting married next month. [1]Congratulations to you on your [2]upcoming wedding! My family and I are so glad that we have been invited to your wedding ceremony! It will be your [3]big day, and I can't wait for that day to come soon!

You have been like my big sister since I was born, and I understand what kind of man you like the most. You like the man who is responsible both at work and at home. [4]Besides, he should be a [5]caring person, who can [6]take care of his family. [7]Furthermore, he should be patient in solving problems, whether big or small. Luckily, you have met a man with all these [8]qualities! He is [9]diligent, considerate, and understanding.

Soon, you will get married to the man of your choice. I believe that you are ready to start a new life. Please accept my best wishes upon your [10]marriage.

Congratulations again!

Love,

Jill

Total: 166 words

Vocabulary & Phrases in Use

1. **congratulation** n. 恭賀
2. **upcoming** adj. 即將發生的
3. **big day** phr. 重要的日子
4. **besides** adv. 而且
5. **caring** adj. 體貼的
6. **take care of** phr. 照顧，照料
7. **furthermore** adv. 而且
8. **quality** n. 特質
9. **diligent** adj. 勤奮的
10. **marriage** n. 婚姻

Writing Tips

1. 本文的開頭 How have you been? 為典型的問候語，類似的用法還有 How are you?、How are things with you? 和 How's it going with you? 等。

2. 本文常見用法有 Congratulations to sb on sth 和 Please accept my best wishes upon sth，可套用在祝賀等類似情境的書信中。

3. 本文的第二段運用不少正面的形容詞描述一個人的特質，例如：responsible、caring、patient、diligent、considerate，以及 understanding，可在描述好友或欽佩某人等類似情境的文章中多加運用。

4. 本文是寫給親人，結尾語可用 With warmest regards、Warm wishes 或 Love 等。

59

27 A Letter About a Worry

你最近有一點煩惱想找你的朋友或同學傾訴，你 (英文名字必須假設為 Michael 或 Amy) 打算寫一封信給他 / 她 (英文名字必須假設為 Tim 或 Sue)，信中請說明你的煩惱為何，並請求對方的幫忙。

請注意：必須使用上述的 Michael 或 Amy 在信末署名，**不得使用自己的真實中文或英文名字**。

Dear Sue,

How are things with you? I am writing this letter to you because something has been troubling me recently. Therefore, I'd like to ask for your advice. Strange to say, recently ¹pimples have cropped up all over my face. Sometimes, I really want to ²squeeze them in order to ³get rid of them. However, I was told that if I squeeze them, this would leave ⁴noticeable ⁵scars on my face. Not knowing what to do, I went to a couple of doctors. The ⁶ointment they ⁷prescribed worked for a while. However, once I stop applying it, the pimples come back again.

⁸Owing to these pimples, I feel embarrassed at school, and I can't even ⁹pluck up the courage to talk to the boy I like. I really need some advice from you as I once noticed that your pimples had disappeared and no scars were left. I would really ¹⁰appreciate it if you can tell me how you solved the problem. Thank you so much!

Best wishes,

Amy

Total: 170 words

Vocabulary & Phrases in Use

1. **pimple** n. 青春痘
2. **squeeze** v. 擠壓
3. **get rid of** phr. 擺脫
4. **noticeable** adj. 明顯的
5. **scar** n. 疤痕
6. **ointment** n. 藥膏

7. **prescribe** v. 開 (藥)
8. **owing to** prep. 由於
9. **pluck up (the) courage to...** phr. 鼓起勇氣做…
10. **appreciate** v. 感激

Writing Tips

1. 本文是寫給朋友，結尾語可用 Best wishes 或 Best regards 等。

2. 本文的結尾 I would really appreciate it... 和 Thank you so much! 可在類似情境的書信中多加運用。

3. 本文常見用法有 strange to say (說來奇怪)、in order to (為了) 和 owing to (由於)，還有被動語態 (I was told...) 和分詞用法 (Not knowing..., I went to...)，可套用在類似情境的文章中。

28 A Letter About a Student Club

你的親友即將跟你就讀同一所高中，詢問你該如何選擇學校的社團，你 (英文名字必須假設為 Sam 或 Joan) 打算回一封信給他／她 (英文名字必須假設為 Paul 或 Emily)，第一段說明你推薦的社團為何，可以舉自己所參加過社團的例子，第二段說明原因。請注意：必須使用上述的 Sam 或 Joan 在信末署名，**不得使用自己的真實中文或英文名字**。

Dear Paul,

It was great to hear from you. You asked me how to choose a ^{1}student club the other day. Our school offers ^{2}a wide range of clubs. You are free to choose the one you like the most. However, I strongly ^{3}recommend that you join the English Speech Club. Now, there are twenty members in the club, including me and the ^{4}club president. We are required to make a speech in English ^{5}in turn once a week. In our club, we provide a friendly environment so that all the members can ^{6}improve their speaking skills without stress.

The club members are all interested in English. Luckily, we have an excellent ^{7}adviser, Mr. Yang, who is one of the English teachers in our school. He trains us to speak English ^{8}properly and ^{9}fluently. So far, I've ^{10}not only improved my English a lot but also gained ^{11}leadership skills. So, what are you waiting for? We welcome you to our club anytime. Tell me about what you think in your next letter. I hope to hear from you soon.

Best regards,

Joan

Total: 182 words

Vocabulary & Phrases in Use

1. **student club** n. 社團
2. **a wide range of** 各式各樣的
3. **recommend** v. 推薦
4. **club president** n. 社長
5. **in turn** phr. 輪流
6. **improve** v. 改善

7. **adviser** n. 顧問
8. **properly** adv. 正確地
9. **fluently** adv. 流利地
10. **not only...but also...** phr.
    不僅…而且…
11. **leadership** n. 領導能力

Writing Tips

1. 本文的開頭 It was great to hear from you. 為典型的問候語，結尾 I hope to hear from you soon. 也是常見用法。

2. 本文第一段所描述的社團活動，可套用在描述最喜歡的學校社團、社團中難忘的回憶或學生時期最喜歡的活動等類似情境的文章中。

3. 本文常見用法有 including A and B (包含 A 和 B)、被動語態 (We are required...) 以及同位語 (adviser, Mr. Yang, who is...)，可在寫作時多加運用。

4. 本文是寫給親友，結尾語可用 Best regards、Best wishes 或 Sincerely 等。

㉙ A Sincere Warning to My Best Friend (101 學測)

你最好的朋友最近迷上電玩，因此常常熬夜，疏忽課業，並受到父母的責罵。你 (英文名字必須假設為 Jack 或 Jill) 打算寫一封信給他 / 她 (英文名字必須假設為 Ken 或 Barbie) ，適當地給予勸告。

請注意：必須使用上述的 Jack 或 Jill 在信末署名，**不得使用自己的真實中文或英文名字**。

Dear Ken,

It has been quite a while since we last played basketball together. Whenever I see you after school, you always rush home. ^{1}As far as I know, you ^{2}are addicted to ^{3}video games and stay up almost every day. Your grades have dropped ^{4}dramatically. I heard that your parents get mad and ^{5}scold you all the time. I'm really ^{6}concerned about you.

^{7}There is no denying that playing video games is exciting. However, I ^{8}advise that you ^{9}regard it as ^{10}nothing but a way to help you relax and ^{11}relieve your tension sometimes. Nevertheless, playing basketball can do the same! Moreover, spending too much time playing video games can have bad effects on both your grades and health, while playing basketball can keep you fit. Do you remember the good times we ^{12}used to have on the basketball court? Why don't you ^{13}cut down on playing the games and come back to the court? I'm looking forward to playing basketball with you soon!

Your friend,

Jack

Total: 168 words

Vocabulary & Phrases in Use

1. **as far as I know** phr.
   據我所知
2. **be addicted to...** 對…入迷
3. **video game** n. 電玩
4. **dramatically** adv. 明顯地
5. **scold** v. 責罵
6. **concerned** adj. 擔憂的
7. **there is no denying that...**
   phr. 無可否認…
8. **advise** v. 建議
9. **regard...as...** 視…為…
10. **nothing but** phr. 只是
11. **relieve one's tension**
    減緩某人的緊張
12. **used to** v. 過去曾經
13. **cut down on sth** phr. 減少…

Writing Tips

1. 本文是寫給朋友，結尾語可用 Your friend 或 Best regards 等。
2. 寫作時適時運用連接詞和慣用語，可讓文章更順暢，例如：
   whenever 及 as far as I know。
3. 本文常見用法有 it has been quite a while since... (自從…有很長一段時間)、be addicted to... (對…入迷)、stay up (熬夜) 和 look forward to (盼望)，可套用在類似情境的文章中。
4. 本文提到籃球場 (basketball court)，還有其他球類運動的場地也可用 court，例如：badminton court (羽球場)、tennis court (網球場)和 volleyball court (排球場)。然而，棒球場及足球場的用法則是baseball field 和 football field。

65

❸❿ An Apology Letter to a Friend (97 學測)

你 (英文名字必須假設為 George 或 Mary) 向朋友 (英文名字必須假設為 Adam 或 Eve) 借了一件相當珍貴的物品，但不慎遺失，一時又買不到替代品。請寫一封信，第一段說明物品遺失的經過，第二段則表達歉意並提出可能的解決方案。

請注意：為避免評分困擾，請使用上述提示的 George 或 Mary 在信末署名，**不得使用自己真實的中文或英文姓名**。

Dear Adam,

    Thank you for lending me the ¹digital ²single lens reflex camera for the activity of the ³Photography Club at our school. This early morning, I went to the mountains with the camera. Your camera was so wonderful that I used it to take many ⁴stunning photos of ⁵sunrise and ⁶mountain scenery. Unfortunately, I lost the camera ⁷by accident on my way home. It was most likely that I left it somewhere on the bus I took home from the mountains. I knew that this camera was important to you as it is a graduation present that your grandfather bought you.

    Though I didn't mean to lose it, there was no excuse for my carelessness. Now, I want to apologize to you and do something to make it up to you. Here is my ⁸proposal. I would try to find a part-time job to make money so that I could ⁹afford to buy you a new one or pay you the equal amount of ¹⁰compensation. Please accept my apology. I hope you can forgive me this time.

Sincerely yours,

Mary

Total: 181 words

Vocabulary & Phrases in Use

1. **digital** adj. 數位的
2. **single lens reflex camera** n. 單眼相機
3. **Photography Club** n. 攝影社
4. **stunning** adj. 極漂亮的
5. **sunrise** n. 日出
6. **mountain scenery** n. 山中景色
7. **by accident** phr. 意外地
8. **proposal** n. 提案
9. **afford** v. 負擔得起
10. **compensation** n. 賠償金

Writing Tips

1. 本文依提示在第一段說明物品遺失的經過，第二段則表達歉意並提出可能的解決方案。寫作時須注意不要離題。

2. 本文的開頭 Thank you for... 可套用在感謝等類似情境的書信中；結尾 Though I didn't mean to..., there was no excuse for... 和 please accept my apology 則可套用在道歉等類似情境的書信中。

3. 本文是寫給朋友，結尾語可用 Sincerely yours、Best wishes 或 Kind regards 等。

4. 寫作時適時運用關係代名詞，可讓文章更精簡，例如：...a graduation present that your grandfather bought...。

5. 本文常見用法有 so...that... (如此⋯以至於⋯)、by accident (意外地) 和 most likely that... (很有可能⋯)，可套用在類似情境的文章中。

31 A Visit to a Doctor

人生病的時候都會去看醫生，西醫或中醫，甚至牙醫。請寫一篇英文作文敘述你個人看醫生的經驗，文分兩段，第一段敘述去看醫生的原因，第二段則描述看醫生的過程、感想等。

When I was little, one day after school, I found myself suffering from a bad headache, a ¹sore throat, and a ²persistent ³cough. I was too weak to do anything. What's worse, I was running a high fever. Therefore, my parents took me to see Dr. Wang at the local ⁴clinic immediately.

While I was at the clinic, I found that Dr. Wang and the nurses there were so warm and caring. Dr. Wang was so patient with me even though I was crying out in pain. At the same time, one of the nurses gave me some cartoon stickers with a smile. Finally, I calmed myself down and listened to Dr. Wang carefully. He told me that I got the flu and had to take medicine four times a day for a week. Furthermore, he suggested that I should take a week's sick leave from school and have a ⁵balanced ⁶diet. Lastly, I was told to ⁷get a flu shot next time. ⁸Thanks to Dr. Wang's ⁹medical treatment, I ¹⁰recovered from the ¹¹illness very soon.

Total: 176 words

Vocabulary & Phrases in Use

1. **sore throat** n. 喉嚨痛
2. **persistent** adj. 不間斷的
3. **cough** n. 咳嗽
4. **clinic** n. 診所
5. **balanced** adj. 均衡的
6. **diet** n. 飲食

7. **get a flu shot** 接種流感疫苗
8. **thanks to** phr. 多虧
9. **medical treatment** n. 治療
10. **recover from** 康復
11. **illness** n. 疾病

Writing Tips

1. 本文以個人看醫生的經驗為主題，時態多以過去式為主。

2. 本文使用許多形容身體不舒服的用詞，例如：bad headache、sore throat、persistent cough、high fever，可套用在描述感冒症狀、過敏等類似情境的文章中。

3. 本文常見用法有 suffer from (患有)，在說明有感冒或其他病症時皆可使用。還有時間副詞 at the same time (同一時間)、finally (最後) 和 lastly (最後)，也可在寫作時多加運用。

4. 另外，本文提到 cartoon sticker (卡通貼紙) 的用法，可在描寫童年經驗等類似情境的文章中多加運用。

32 One Thing I've Learned from My Classmate

我們生活週遭的人，同學或朋友，對我們都有某種程度的影響。
請寫一篇英文作文，第一段敘述一件同學令你印象深刻的事，第
二段說明這件事對你的影響。

When I was a junior high school student, one of my classmates, Vivian, [1]had a great influence on me. Vivian was a shy and quiet girl in class. Sometimes, I noticed that she didn't leave the classroom right away like other classmates did after school. At first, I [2]wondered why she stayed in the classroom, but I didn't think much about it. One day after school, she stayed in the classroom as usual, and I decided to see what would happen next. After ten minutes, it surprised me that she [3]swept the floor, took out the garbage, and then checked if all the windows were closed.

Her action [4]inspired me to do the same. I [5]praised Vivian for her [6]thoughtfulness and sense of [7]responsibility. She just smiled and said, "It's really nothing. I would like to [8]provide a clean and safe environment for our classmates to start a new day." Since then, I've been taking part in voluntary work [9]as long as I have time after school. Vivian really [10]impressed me, and I have to thank her for this important lesson she taught me.

Total: 184 words

1. **have an influence on...**
   對…產生影響

2. **wonder** v. 疑惑

3. **sweep** v. 打掃

4. **inspire** v. 激勵

5. **praise sb for sth**
   因為某事而稱讚某人

6. **thoughtfulness** n. 體貼

7. **responsibility** n. 責任

8. **provide** v. 提供

9. **as long as** phr. 只要

10. **impress** v. 使印象深刻

Writing Tips

1. 本文以「令人印象深刻的事」和「對自己的影響」為主架構，時態以過去式為主，文章內容可套用在描述朋友的特質或描述最好的朋友等類似情境的文章中。

2. 本文常見用法有 It's really nothing.，可用來當作謙虛地接受誇獎時的回應。

3. 本文使用 if 表示「是否」，例如：...she...checked if all the windows were closed.。在句中表示「是否」的 if 也可用 whether 替換。

33 A Great Person in Human History

讀過中外歷史，人類史上有無數偉大的人物，有發明家、藝術家、政治家，甚至作家。請寫一篇英文作文，第一段介紹一位你所知道的歷史人物，第二段則說明其貢獻。

Thomas Edison is one of the greatest [1]inventors of all time. Not accepted by his [2]bad-tempered teacher, Edison had very little [3]schooling. In addition, he was [4]hearing-impaired when he was a child. Instead of giving up on him, his parents educated him at home. As for Edison, he did not give up on himself, either. He once told himself, "Be [5]courageous. Have [6]faith! [7]Go forward." He had such a strong desire for knowledge that he finished reading almost all the books in the local library.

Throughout his life, Edison patented over one thousand [8]inventions that greatly influenced people's lives. For example, the light bulb is his greatest invention. Because of the light bulb, we can work, read, and even play [9]after dark. In conclusion, Edison [10]made a great contribution to the whole world, and I admire him the most.

Total: 139 words

1. **inventor** n. 發明家
2. **bad-tempered** adj. 脾氣差的
3. **schooling** n. 學校教育
4. **hearing-impaired** adj.
   聽覺受損的
5. **courageous** adj. 勇敢的

6. **faith** n. 信心
7. **go forward** phr. 前進
8. **invention** n. 發明
9. **after dark** phr. 天黑後
10. **make a contribution to...**
    對…有貢獻

1. 本文介紹歷史人物，以描述「歷史人物」和「其貢獻」為主架構，主要時態是過去式，但陳述一般事實須用現在式。

2. 本文開門見山地在第一句點出要介紹的人物，然後先簡短地描述生平後，再敘述其貢獻，這是最常用且直接的寫法。

3. 本文常見用法有 give up on sb (放棄某人) 和 make a contribution to... (對…有貢獻)，以及分詞用法 (Not accepted by..., Edison had...) 和從屬連接詞 (He had such a strong desire...that he finished reading...)，可在類似情境的文章中多加運用。

4. 本文使用複合形容詞 bad-tempered 表示 「脾氣差的」，也可用 short-tempered 或 hot-tempered 替換。另外，hearing-impaired (聽覺受損的) 為由名詞 + 形容詞組合而成的複合字，類似字詞還有 vision-impaired (視覺受損的) 等。

③④ The Best Tourist Attraction in Town

每個人對自己生活的地方都有相當程度的了解與認識，包括其中的餐廳、商店、電影院等。請寫一篇英文作文，第一段介紹你所居住的地區最值得推薦的景點，第二段則說明其特色和優點。

Tainan, the city in which I live, is the first planned city in Taiwan. Thus, Tainan is full of ¹historic sites. Among all the historic sites, I would like to introduce my favorite one, Tainan Confucius Temple. It was built in 1665 and was once the highest ²educational institution. ³To this day, this temple ⁴remains intact and has become a famous ⁵tourist attraction.

Step through the gate into the great ⁶courtyard, and you are sure to enjoy the beautiful ⁷architecture and serene ⁸atmosphere in this ⁹ancient temple. Furthermore, you can see trees everywhere and ¹⁰flocks of birds fly ¹¹overhead sometimes. Every September, a special traditional ceremony is held ¹²in memory of Confucius. In addition, this ancient temple also ¹³serves as a ¹⁴recreational spot for the locals. People go there to walk and chat with each other. A trip to Tainan wouldn't be complete without a tour of Tainan Confucius Temple. It is definitely worth paying a visit.

Total: 157 words

Vocabulary & Phrases in Use

1. **historic site** n. 古蹟
2. **educational institution** n. 教育機構
3. **to this day** phr. 至今
4. **remain** v. 仍然是
5. **tourist attraction** n. 旅遊景點
6. **courtyard** n. 庭院
7. **architecture** n. 建築
8. **atmosphere** n. 氣氛
9. **ancient** adj. 古老的
10. **flock** n. (鳥) 群
11. **overhead** adv. 在空中
12. **in memory of sb** phr. 紀念某人
13. **serve as** 作為
14. **recreational spot** n. 休閒場所

Writing Tips

1. 本文介紹自己居住的地方，主要時態用現在式；但若敘述過去狀況，則用過去式。主要架構為：⑴最值得推薦的地點。⑵其特色和優點。本文內容可套用在描述最喜歡或最想去的地方等類似情境的文章中；也可套用在第 35 篇 "How I Spent My Summer Vacation" 這樣的作文題目中，敘述自己去孔廟的故事。

2. 本文常見用法有 be full of (充滿)、in memory of sb (紀念某人) 和 it is worth V-ing (值得…)，以及 wouldn't be complete without... (沒有…就不完整)，還有關係代名詞 (Tainan, the city in which I live, is the first...) 和被動式 (a special traditional ceremony is held...)，可在寫作時多加運用。同時記得適時運用轉折語，讓文章更流暢，例如：furthermore 和 in addition。

35 How I Spent My Summer Vacation

請以 "How I Spent My Summer Vacation" 為題 ， 寫一篇英文作文，第一段描述你某個暑假所從事的活動，第二段說明你從活動中獲得的助益或感想。

    Every student looks forward to the coming of summer vacation, and I'm [1]no exception. Last summer, I decided to learn how to swim, so I [2]signed up for a swimming class in the community center. After signing up, I was so excited that I couldn't wait for my first swimming class to come. During my first [3]session, my swimming [4]instructor suggested that I get into the pool immediately. However, I felt too nervous to dive into the water. Fortunately, [5]with the help of the instructor, I could [6]float on my back. "Good job," said the instructor. I was encouraged by his words and made up my mind to learn to swim well. In the [7]following weeks, I not only [8]conquered my fear of water but also swam a long distance [9]smoothly.

    That's how I spent my last summer vacation. Now, I go swimming [10]regularly, usually three times a week, since I find that swimming can help me relax and also [11]maintain health. In conclusion, making good use of summer vacation can be quite beneficial, even after a new semester starts!

Total: 180 words

Vocabulary & Phrases in Use

1. **no exception** phr. 也不例外
2. **sign up for** phr. 報名參加
3. **session** n. 一節課
4. **instructor** n. 教練
5. **with the help of...** 有…的幫忙
6. **float** v. 漂浮
7. **following** adj. (時間上) 接著的
8. **conquer** v. 戰勝
9. **smoothly** adv. 順利地
10. **regularly** adv. 規律地
11. **maintain** v. 保持

Writing Tips

1. 寫作時，內容盡量以一個活動為發展主題，避免過多的主題出現在同一篇短文中，以便讓文章針對一個主題做發展並描述細節。本文內容可套用在 How I learned... 等類似情境的文章中。

2. 本文運用 after signing up...、I couldn't wait...、I was encouraged...、I not only...、now... 等描述過程，可套用在描述學習任何一種新的事物或運動等類似情境的文章中。

3. 本文常見用法有 look forward to (盼望)、the coming of... (…的來臨)、can't wait for... (等不及…) 和 make up one's mind to... (下定決心做…)，可在類似情境的文章中多加運用。

36 The First Time I Spoke English

請以 "The First Time I Spoke English" 為題寫一篇英文作文，文分兩段，第一段描述第一次開口說英語的經驗，第二段談該經驗帶給你的感受。

  The first time I spoke English was when I was in high school. One night, I met a young American ¹exchange student from my school on a bus. He didn't know where to ²get off, and no one on the bus could ³give him a hand. Though I usually did well on English tests, I had never used English ⁴in real life. However, I decided to help him out. I asked him where he wanted to go and told him the right stop to get off. During our conversation, we even ⁵chatted ⁶a little bit.

  Although I was really ⁷nervous ⁸the whole time when I talked to him, the experience was surprisingly ⁹pleasant! Besides, I was really happy that I could finally use what I had learned from school for real ¹⁰communication and for helping people. As a result, I have enjoyed learning English more and become more confident in speaking English from then on.

Total: 155 words

Vocabulary & Phrases in Use

1. **exchange student** n. 交換學生
2. **get off** phr. 下 (車)
3. **give sb a hand** phr. 幫助某人
4. **in real life** phr. 在現實生活中
5. **chat** v. 聊天，閒聊
6. **a little bit** phr. 稍微
7. **nervous** adj. 緊張的
8. **the whole time** phr. 一直
9. **pleasant** adj. 令人愉快的
10. **communication** n. 溝通

Writing Tips

1. 本文將題目 "The First Time I Spoke English" 運用在開頭的主題句，並依照提示分成兩段撰寫短文，主要內容分為個人的「經驗」和「感受」。

2. 本文第一段的故事可用在描述第一次幫助別人的經驗或是最難忘的經驗等類似情境的文章中，第一段的第四句和第五句 Though I...However, ... 可在描述做某事時缺乏經驗卻成功等類似情境的文章中多加運用。

3. 寫作時可適時運用連接詞和時間副詞，讓文章更順暢，像是第一段用 though (雖然) 表示語氣轉折，以及用 during our conversation (在我們交談的期間) 承接前句語意。

4. 本文常見用法有 give sb a hand 和 help sb out，皆可表示幫助某人，可在寫作時多加運用。

③ My Favorite Type of TV Program

請以 "My Favorite Type of TV Program" 為題，寫一篇英文作文，文分兩段，第一段說明你最喜歡看的電視節目種類，簡單介紹其內容，第二段說明你喜歡這類電視節目的理由。

I enjoy watching TV in my free time. Of all the TV programs, those about travel are my favorites. Popular television travel programs can be [1]broadcasted for many years. They provide us with lots of information about different cultures, food, and [2]tourism [3]worldwide. There can be many [4]hosts [5]participating in a TV show, introducing [6]a wide variety of [7]tourist resorts.

There are three reasons why I enjoy watching travel programs so much. First, many show hosts are funny and [8]entertaining. I always laugh while watching these shows. Some foreign hosts can impress me with their unique [9]sense of humor and fluent Chinese. Some of the hosts can even be [10]awarded the Golden Bell Award. Second, these programs help me gain lots of useful knowledge about different cultures of the world. By watching these interesting programs, I've [11]broadened my horizons. What's more, some travel programs are in Chinese, Taiwanese, and English. I could learn some English as well. [12]All in all, travel programs are my favorite TV programs.

Total: 168 words

Vocabulary & Phrases in Use

1. **broadcast** v. 播放
2. **tourism** n. 旅遊業
3. **worldwide** adv. 全世界地
4. **host** n. 主持人
5. **participate in** 參與
6. **a wide variety of** 各式各樣的
7. **tourist resort** n. 旅遊勝地
8. **entertaining** adj.
   有娛樂效果的
9. **sense of humor** n. 幽默感
10. **award** v. 授與
11. **broaden one's horizons**
    拓展某人的視野
12. **all in all** phr. 總而言之

Writing Tips

1. 本文依提示分成兩段撰寫，主要內容包括：⑴個人喜歡的電視節目種類。⑵喜歡的理由。注意喜歡的理由必須清楚且能說服人。

2. 本文第二段的內容可套用在描述未來想從事的行業及理由等類似情境的文章中；其中的部分內容也可在描述如何學習英文等類似情境的文章中多加運用。

3. 本文常見用法有 a wide variety of (各式各樣的) 、 impress sb with sth (某事使某人感到印象深刻) 和 broaden one's horizons (拓展某人的視野)，可在寫作時多加運用。

③8 My Personal Experience of Learning...

任何人都有過學習某種事物的經驗，請以 "My Personal Experience of Learning..." 為題寫一篇英文作文，第一段描述你學習某項事物的經過及方法，第二段說明你的學習心得或感想。

[1]At the age of ten, I wanted to own a bicycle, though I didn't know how to ride one. [2]Later on, my parents bought me a [3]brand new bike and taught me some [4]techniques of riding. I still remember the day I saw my little red shiny bike, which came with two [5]side wheels. I got on my bike and tried to move forward the first time. To my surprise, I could ride it smoothly. Then, I decided to ride it again without side wheels. However, when I [6]struggled to keep my [7]balance on the bike, I fell off it many times. My parents didn't come forward to help me but encouraged me to try again.

After many [8]failures, I could finally ride my bike successfully [9]without the assistance of my parents as well as the side wheels. How happy and satisfied I was when I could ride my bicycle [10]on my own! I was proud that I didn't give up and kept learning so that I made it at last. As the saying goes, "Where there's a will there's a way!"

Total: 182 words

Vocabulary & Phrases in Use

1. **at the age of...** phr. …歲時
2. **later on** phr. 之後
3. **brand new** adj. 全新的
4. **technique** n. 技巧
5. **side wheel** n. 輔助輪
6. **struggle** v. 努力
7. **balance** n. 平衡
8. **failure** n. 失敗
9. **without the assistance of...** 不靠…的協助
10. **on one's own** phr. 靠自己

Writing Tips

1. 本文內容描寫個人經驗，時態須用過去式，並依提示撰寫文章，主要內容以學習某事物的「經過」和「方法」為主。

2. 本文常見用法有 fall off... (從…跌落)，還有關係代名詞 (...my little red shiny bike, which came with...)，可在類似情境的文章中多加運用。

3. 本文大部分的內容可套用在第 35 篇 "How I Spent My Summer Vacation" 等類似情境的文章中，只要將開頭的 At the age of ten 改成 Last summer，並略作潤飾即可。

39 I Want to Be...

請寫一篇英文作文說明你的志願,第一段敘述你未來想從事什麼行業並說明原因,第二段則說明你打算如何實現你的志願。

I want to be a teacher in the future due to my personal experience. When I was eleven years old, I found the school lessons boring, and I ¹had difficulty ²concentrating on my studies. Some people ³thought of me as a ⁴naughty child. However, my teacher, Ms. Lin, didn't give up on me. She ⁵kept on ⁶encouraging me to learn to concentrate in class. Besides, she lent me many interesting books to help me ⁷develop a habit of reading and learn to read for enjoyment. Furthermore, she even stayed in class after school to help me and other students who ⁸have problems with their schoolwork. Thanks to her effort and encouragement, I did improve myself a lot. Therefore, I want to be a teacher to spark their interest in studying.

Since I've made up my mind to be a teacher, I will study hard to gain as much knowledge as possible and earn a ⁹teacher's certificate. With my ¹⁰expertise and patience, I believe I will become a good teacher in the future.

Total: 172 words

Vocabulary & Phrases in Use

1. **have difficulty + V-ing**
   做⋯有困難

2. **concentrate on...** phr. 專心⋯

3. **think of sb as...** 視某人為⋯

4. **naughty** adj. 頑皮的

5. **keep on + V-ing** phr. 持續⋯

6. **encourage** v. 鼓勵

7. **develop a habit of...**
   養成⋯習慣

8. **have problems with...**
   在⋯上有困難

9. **teacher's certificate** n.
   教師證照

10. **expertise** n. 專業知識

Writing Tips

1. 本文以自己的志願為題，內容包括「敘述原因」(多以過去時態為主) 以及「計畫達成理想」(現在式和未來式)。

2. 本文常見用法有 due to (由於)、have difficulty + V-ing (做⋯有困難)、concentrate on... (專心於⋯) 和 give up on sb (放棄某人)，以及在逗點前後使用同位語，帶出某人的職業和姓名，例如：...my teacher, Ms. Lin...，可在寫作時多加運用。

3. 本文部分內容可放在敘述求學時期最喜歡的老師或是印象最深刻的一件事等類似情境的文章中。

⑩ Pocket Money

請寫一篇英文短文，第一段說明你有沒有零用錢，並敘述你認為每個月零用錢要多少才合理，第二段說明你規劃如何支配運用你的零用錢。

I have some ^{1}pocket money, part of which is allowance I get from my parents, and the rest of which is earned from my part-time job. The ^{2}ideal amount of pocket money for me should be three thousand NT dollars every month. The money would be ^{3}divided into three parts: ^{4}one for food, another for ^{5}social life, and the other for books and magazines.

^{6}Normally, I spend a ^{7}fixed amount of money, which is one thousand dollars, on food a month because I pay for my lunches at the school ^{8}cafeteria sometimes and buy light ^{9}snacks ^{10}occasionally. I have breakfast and dinner at home; therefore, I only have to spend money on my lunch. Another one thousand dollars is spent on social life. I usually hang out with my friends on weekends. Sometimes, we go to the movies, and sometimes we go swimming or hiking in the mountains. The last one thousand dollars is spent on books and magazines. As a student, I read comic books, ^{11}romantic novels, or travel magazines to ^{12}spice up my life. In conclusion, this is how I would spend my pocket money per month.

Total: 189 words

Vocabulary & Phrases in Use

1. **pocket money** n. 零用錢

2. **ideal** adj. 理想的

3. **divide** v. 分開

4. **one..., another..., the other...**
   一個…，一個…，另一個…

5. **social** adj. 社交的

6. **normally** adv. 正常情況下

7. **fixed** adj. 固定的

8. **cafeteria** n. 自助餐廳

9. **snack** n. 點心

10. **occasionally** adv. 偶爾

11. **romantic novel** n. 言情小說

12. **spice up...** phr. 增添…的趣味

Writing Tips

1. 本文為表達自我意見的文章，多以議論的角度出發。先按照指示說明自己有沒有零用錢，並以主題句 (topic sentence) 提出自己的立場 The ideal amount of pocket money for me should be...every month.，描述每個月零用錢要多少才合理，接著利用自身實例來支持論點 (supporting details)，敘述如何運用這些錢，以便寫作時不易離題。

2. 本文常見用法有 divide into... (分成…) 、 one..., another..., the other... (一個…，一個…，另一個…) 、 spend money on sth (花錢在…) 和 on weekends (週末)，可在類似情境的文章中多加運用。

㊶ My Favorite Book

請寫一篇英文作文介紹你最喜愛的一本書。文分兩段，第一段敘述這本書的內容及特色，第二段說明這本書對你的影響。

　　My favorite book is *The Present*. It tells the story of a young man [1]looking for the true meaning of life. At first, this man was upset and frustrated because of the difficulties he met in his life. Then, he visited an old man. The old man told the young man that if he changed the way he viewed life, he would find the happiness he longed for. After the young man did what he was told to do, he realized that "the present moment" was the present, not the past nor the future. [2]Only when he [3]focused on what he was doing [4]at the moment could he [5]truly enjoy himself. This led him to success and happiness.

　　This story has made a strong [6]impression on me. I now do understand if I'm stuck in the past or worrying about the future, I will fail to [7]seize the moment. In other words, I should [8]live in the present. Therefore, whenever I feel [9]distressed or [10]confused, I always think of *The Present* and the valuable lesson this book has taught me.

Total: 180 words

Vocabulary & Phrases in Use

1. **look for** phr. 尋找
2. **only when...** 只有當…
3. **focus on** phr. 專注於
4. **at the moment** phr. 當下
5. **truly** adv. 確實地

6. **impression** n. 印象
7. **seize** v. 把握 (時機)
8. **live in the present** 活在當下
9. **distressed** adj. 煩惱的
10. **confused** adj. 困惑的

Writing Tips

1. 本文以最喜歡的一本書為主題，通常的寫法為第一段簡述書的內容及特色，第二段說明讀完之後所學到的東西，並敘述對個人的影響。本文內容可套用在描述影響個人最深的一本書或是大家都該讀的一本書等類似情境的文章中。

2. 本文常見用法有 long for (渴望)、only when... (只有當…)、make a strong impression on sb (讓某人印象深刻) 和 live in the present (活在當下)。並適時運用副詞，例如：then 和 therefore。

❹ Finding Mr. or Ms. Right Through the Internet

透過網路結交朋友是一件相當普遍的事 ，請以 It's (not) an ideal way to find Mr. or Ms. Right through the Internet. 為開頭寫一篇英文作文。文分兩段，第一段說明你覺得在網路上找理想伴侶適合或不適合的理由，第二段則闡述你認為理想伴侶該有哪些條件。

It's not an ideal way to find Mr. or Ms. Right through the Internet. [1]Internet dating seems like a great idea, but how can you know for sure the person you meet online is the right person? The main concern over meeting someone online is one's own safety. The reason is simple. How do you know if the person you meet online is the same one you meet in person or what kind of personality he or she really has? Therefore, it is necessary to be very careful with [2]online dating.

The following things can be [3]taken into account when you consider who is right for you. First of all, Mr. or Ms. Right should be [4]independent enough to [5]support himself or herself and be responsible for his or her family. Second, Mr. or Ms. Right should [6]respect you. When a man respects a woman, he is less likely to [7]betray or [8]mistreat her, and vice versa. [9]Last but not least, Mr. or Ms. Right should make you happy. The person who can make you smile easily should be the best one for you. If you [10]keep all these qualities in mind, you won't [11]go wrong with finding your Mr. or Ms. Right.

Total: 203 words

Vocabulary & Phrases in Use

1. **Internet dating** n. 網路約會
2. **online dating** n. 網路約會
3. **take...into account** phr. 將…列入考慮
4. **independent** adj. 獨立的
5. **support** v. 養活
6. **respect** v. 尊敬
7. **betray** v. 背叛
8. **mistreat** v. 虐待
9. **last but not least** phr. 最後但同樣重要的
10. **keep...in mind** phr. 將…記在心中
11. **go wrong** phr. 出問題，失敗

Writing Tips

1. 本文以 It's (not) an ideal way to find Mr. or Ms. Right through the Internet. 為開頭，文分兩段，第一段說明不適合在網路上找理想伴侶的理由，第二段闡述哪些條件是理想伴侶該有的。

2. 本文第二段的部分內容描述一個人的特質，可套用在描述自己親友或是欽佩某個人等類似情境的文章中。

3. 本文常見用法有 for sure (確定)、in person (親自) 和 take...into account (將…列入考慮)，以及 vice versa (反之亦然)。

43 A Story About Internet Dating

透過網路結交朋友是一件相當普遍的事，也常見於新聞報導，你有聽說過相關的故事嗎？你自己或親友有沒有親身的經驗呢？請以 It's (not) an ideal way to find Mr. or Ms. Right through the Internet. 為開頭寫一篇英文作文，描述一個透過網路結交朋友的故事。

It's not an ideal way to find Mr. or Ms. Right through the Internet. One of my friends, Ben, has a bad experience with online dating. Last month, he found a charming girl, Sally, on a dating website. He was so ¹fascinated with her that he desired to have a date with her.

Last Saturday evening, they finally met for dinner. ²In the beginning, they had a good chat. Then, after a while, she began to tell him that her dad was suffering from a serious illness in the hospital. Her mom was so ³exhausted from taking care of him. Furthermore, it ⁴cost ⁵a fortune to cure him. Therefore, she ⁶begged Ben to ⁷lend her fifty thousand NT dollars and promised him that she would return the money afterward. At that moment, he felt ⁸sympathy for her, so he lent her the money immediately. However, he couldn't find the girl anymore from then on. He was so shocked that such a charming girl should ⁹turn out to be a ¹⁰scammer. In a word, finding an ideal partner through the Internet isn't as safe as people imagine.

Total: 186 words

Vocabulary & Phrases in Use

1. **fascinated** adj. 著迷的
2. **in the beginning** phr. 起初
3. **exhausted** adj. 精疲力盡的
4. **cost sth to + V** 花 (錢) 做…
5. **a fortune** n. 一大筆錢
6. **beg sb to + V** 懇求某人做…
7. **lend** v. 借給，借出
8. **sympathy** n. 同情
9. **turn out** phr. 結果是
10. **scammer** n. 詐欺者

Writing Tips

1. 本文以 It's (not) an ideal way to find Mr. or Ms. Right through the Internet. 為開頭，接下來運用實際例子來支持自己的論點；敘述過去的事實必須用過去式時態。

2. 本文常見用法有 have a date with sb (與某人約會)、in the beginning (剛開始時，起初)、after a while (過一會兒)、take care of (照顧) 和 from then on (從那時起)，以及運用 ...not as...as... (不如…一樣…) 表示兩件事物程度不相當，例如：...finding an ideal partner through the Internet isn't as safe as people imagine. ，可在寫作時多加運用。

3. 本文內容可套用在敘述網路詐騙或談論網路安全等類似情境的文章中。

44 Stray Dogs

流浪狗在街頭的情景對人們而言並不陌生，請以 "Stray Dogs" 為題寫一篇英文作文，文分兩段，第一段敘述你對流浪狗的觀察或看法，第二段闡述你認為應如何面對該項問題。

In Taiwan, stray dogs can be seen almost everywhere. Many of them are ¹abandoned pets. They are on the streets, around the corners, or sometimes even right outside our doors. Without proper handling, they may make noise, ²chase ³vehicles, or even bite people. It is a problem that we can't ignore or ⁴turn away from.

In my opinion, the government can do two things to solve the problem of stray dogs. First, ⁵chips ⁶containing ways to reach the owners should be ⁷implanted in every pet dog. In this way, once the dog is lost or, ⁸worse still, abandoned, the government can easily ⁹locate its owner and hold them responsible for their actions, such as fining those who abandon their pet dogs. Second, the government should encourage people to adopt stray dogs instead of buying new ones. For example, those who adopt stray dogs would receive an ¹⁰allowance. Hopefully, with these two methods, this problem might gradually be overcome, and no stray dogs would be seen again on the street!

Total: 169 words

1. **abandoned** adj. 被拋棄的
2. **chase** v. 追逐
3. **vehicle** n. 車輛
4. **turn away from...** phr. 對⋯置之不理
5. **chip** n. 晶片
6. **contain** v. 包含
7. **implant** v. 植入
8. **worse still** phr. 更糟糕的是
9. **locate sb** 找出某人的準確位置
10. **allowance** n. 津貼

1. 此類表達自我意見的文章，多以議論的角度出發。文分兩段，第一段先提出自己的想法 (藉由親身經驗或觀察)，第二段再進一步提出合理的解決方法。
2. 本文提出兩點解決流浪狗問題的辦法，第二段以 First,...such as...Second,...For example,... 的結構，先敘述方法，再舉例詳加解釋，使讀者易於理解。
3. 本文常見用法有被動式 (can be seen) 和關係代名詞 (...those who...)。

⑮ Friends

朋友在我們人生中扮演了重要的角色，請以 "Friends" 為題寫一篇英文作文，文分兩段，第一段闡述好朋友的定義，第二段舉出實例，說明好朋友曾經如何幫助過你。

Besides parents and other family members, friends are those we [1]depend on most heavily in our lives. Good friends are good listeners. They have the patience to listen to us and understand the reasons why we have done certain things. [2]Moreover, good friends provide useful advice [3]at the right time.

I have a friend, May, who has the qualities above. I was once [4]in conflict with another classmate at school. When I was [5]waiting in line for my turn to get my [6]serving of lunch, one of my classmates [7]cut in line suddenly. At that time, I shouted angrily, which shocked other classmates. Luckily, May gave me a pat on the back. She told me she totally understood how I felt, but I shouldn't have [8]reacted that way. Therefore, I took her advice and then apologized to my classmate. I [9]was thankful to May [for] being [10]straightforward and advising me against reacting badly.

Total: 153 words

Vocabulary & Phrases in Use

1. **depend on** phr. 依靠
2. **moreover** adv. 此外
3. **at the right time** 在對的時間
4. **in conflict with...** phr.
   和…起衝突
5. **wait in line** phr. 排隊
6. **serving** n. (食物) 一份
7. **cut in line** phr. 插隊
8. **react** v. 反應
9. **be thankful to sb for sth**
   感謝某人某事
10. **straightforward** adj. 坦率的

Writing Tips

1. 此類文章多以論述為主，表達自己看法，文分兩段，主要內容分成：(1)定義何謂好朋友。(2)舉例說明自身的經驗。

2. 本文運用 heavily 這個副詞來修飾 depend on，描述十分倚重和相當依靠。

3. 本文常見用法有關係代名詞的省略 (friends are those we depend on...)，以及 wait in line (排隊)、cut in line (插隊)、give sb a pat on sth (輕拍某人某處) 和 be thankful to sb for sth (感謝某人某事)。

46 An Idol

年輕人或多或少都有自己的偶像，可能是歌手、演員、運動員等等。請以 "An Idol" 為題寫一篇英文作文，第一段描述一位你崇拜的偶像，第二段說明崇拜的原因。

As the first Asian [1]athlete to win the [2]championship in a super [3]marathon, Lin Yi-Chieh (Kevin Lin) has inspired many people in Taiwan. When he was a student, he trained himself hard for the race. Sometimes, he ran as far as thirty kilometers every day in the early morning. After many years of hard work, he still sticks to his dream and never gives up.

[4]Regardless of many hardships, he always manages to finish the [5]competition. It reminds me of what Napoleon once [6]declared, "[7]Victory belongs to the most [8]persevering." [9]Indeed, he won his own victory through many super marathons and has become a famous star in Taiwan. He [10]earnestly [11]advocated the [12]concept: "I believe I can." in a TV commercial. He also encourages the young to be brave and dedicate themselves to their work and society. In a word, his [13]extraordinary concentration to [14]overcome all the [15]obstacles has left a lasting impression on me.

Total: 155 words

Vocabulary & Phrases in Use

1. **athlete** n. 運動員
2. **championship** n. 冠軍
3. **marathon** n. 馬拉松
4. **regardless of** phr. 不管
5. **competition** n. 比賽
6. **declare** v. 宣稱
7. **victory** n. 勝利
8. **persevering** adj. 不屈不撓的
9. **indeed** adv. 確實地
10. **earnestly** adv. 真誠地
11. **advocate** v. 提倡
12. **concept** n. 概念
13. **extraordinary** adj. 非凡的
14. **overcome** v. 克服
15. **obstacle** n. 障礙

Writing Tips

1. 本文主要著重於「自己崇拜的偶像」及「崇拜的理由」，其內容描述一個人的特質，運用不少正面的形容詞或描述方式，可套用在欽佩某個人或描述親友等類似情境的文章中。

2. 本文常見用法有 many years of hard work (長年的努力)、stick to sth (堅持做…)、remind sb of sth (提醒某人某事)、belong to (屬於) 以及 dedicate oneself to... (致力於…)，可在類似情境的文章中多加運用。

47 The Garbage Problem

垃圾減量是當前各國都相當重視的問題。請寫一篇英文作文，第一段說明垃圾增加的原因，第二段提出減少垃圾的方法。

Most countries in the world are facing the garbage problem. With the ¹population ²explosion and rising ³living standards, it is not surprising that garbage would increase ⁴rapidly. In order to reduce the amount of garbage, the government should enact regulations on the garbage problem. In my opinion, there are two possible ways to ⁵tackle the garbage problem.

To begin with, the government should encourage people to sort the garbage and recycle it. The concept of recycling should be taught at school as well as to the public. Therefore, ⁶garbage cans should be ⁷labeled clearly for people to see at a glance. In addition, the government should ⁸announce that people should use only ⁹designated garbage bags that come with high trash collection ¹⁰fees. In this way, people may think twice before throwing the garbage away ¹¹at will. If these measures are taken, the garbage problems can gradually be decreased in the future.

Total: 151 words

Vocabulary & Phrases in Use

1. **population** n. 人口
2. **explosion** n. 激增
3. **living standards** n. 生活水準
4. **rapidly** adv. 迅速地
5. **tackle** v. 應付
6. **garbage can** n. 垃圾桶

7. **label** v. 用標籤標明
8. **announce** v. 宣布
9. **designated garbage bag** n. 專用垃圾袋
10. **fee** n. 費用
11. **at will** phr. 隨意地

Writing Tips

1. 本文分為兩段，第一段說明垃圾增加的原因，表明論點，第二段提出垃圾減量的可能方法，其中部分內容 (sort、recycle、garbage bag、trash collection fee) 可套用在環境保護等類似情境的文章中。

2. 本文常見用法有 population explosion (人口激增)、rising living standards (提高的生活水準)、sort the garbage (垃圾分類) 和 think twice (仔細思考)，可在論述環保議題時多加運用。

48 On My Way to School

在上學途中，也許你是坐車、走路或騎車，這段路程對你而言有什麼感受呢？請以此為題寫一篇英文作文。文分兩段，第一段敘述你上學途中所觀察到的人事物，第二段則提出你的看法。

Every day, I go to school by bus. I usually see old ladies of my grandmother's age. Many of them wear working ¹outfits, heading for a factory ²nearby. I enjoy hearing them share their own life stories. Sometimes, they talk about their difficulties at home. Sometimes, they ³complain about their ⁴hardships in life. But, ⁵no matter what happens to them, they always encourage ⁶one another to work hard and enjoy themselves. Regardless of the heavy ⁷workloads, they still take a very ⁸optimistic view toward their work and lives.

On my way to school, I realize a few things. Those old ladies have worked so hard possibly in order to relieve their children of financial burdens. Therefore, the young should show more respect and care for their elderly parents. ⁹As for the old ladies' conversations, they are full of ¹⁰words of wisdom. No matter how heavy their workloads are, the old ladies are still content with what they have in life. Their positive attitude toward life impresses me a lot.

Total: 169 words

1. **outfit** n. 全套服裝
2. **nearby** adv. 在附近
3. **complain** v. 抱怨
4. **hardship** n. 困難
5. **no matter what...** phr. 無論…

6. **one another** pron. 互相
7. **workload** n. 工作量
8. **optimistic** adj. 樂觀的
9. **as for** phr. 至於
10. **words of wisdom** n. 金玉良言

Writing Tips

1. 本文分為兩段，主要內容分成：(1)上學途中所見所聞。(2)對所見之事的看法。

2. 本文常見用法有 complain about sth (抱怨某事)、heavy workload (沉重的工作量)、care for sb (照顧)、be full of (充滿) 和 words of wisdom (金玉良言)，並有分詞用法 (Many of them wear..., heading...) 和連接詞 no matter what... (無論…)，可在寫作時多加運用。

49 The Difficulties I Have with Learning...

請寫一篇英文作文，文分兩段，第一段寫出你學習的過程中所遇到的困難，第二段說明處理這項困難的經過及其結果。

As a student growing up in the ^{1}countryside, I ^{2}considered learning English one of the ^{3}toughest things in the world. Of the four language skills, listening was the most difficult one for me. Although I tried my best to pass the English tests, I only got low grades in the listening part. I felt so frustrated and almost gave up.

Luckily, my cousin, Beatrice, ^{4}majored in English at university and gave me some useful tips on sharpening my English skills. She suggested that I should ^{5}subscribe to an English magazine and listen to its radio programs every day. The program usually began with a small talk, which was the most difficult part for me. Therefore, I ^{6}recorded that part and played it repeatedly. ^{7}Jotting down unfamiliar words, I ^{8}looked them up in a dictionary. I spent a lot of time listening to English programs and practicing a lot as a daily ^{9}routine. Little by little, my listening skill has gradually improved, and I ^{10}got a perfect score on the English test last time.

Total: 173 words

Vocabulary & Phrases in Use

1. **countryside** n. 鄉間
2. **consider** v. 認為
3. **tough** adj. 艱難的
4. **major in** phr. 主修
5. **subscribe to** phr. 訂閱

6. **record** v. 錄音
7. **jot down** phr. 匆忙記下
8. **look sth up** phr. 查閱…
9. **routine** n. 慣例
10. **get a perfect score** 得滿分

Writing Tips

1. 本文描述過去的經驗，因此以過去式為主。文分兩段，主要內容分成：(1)學習過程中的困難。(2)處理困難的方法及結果。此類文章通常將重點放在第二段，即解決問題的方法，所以第二段會比第一段的敘述長一些。

2. 本文常見用法有 get low grades (得低分)、give up (放棄)、small talk (閒聊)、daily routine (日常生活) 和 get a perfect score (得滿分)，還有關係代名詞 (...a small talk, which was...) 以及分詞用法 (Jotting down..., I looked...)，並適時運用連接詞和副詞，讓文章更流暢，例如：although、luckily。

3. 本文部分內容可和第 35 篇 "How I Spent My Summer Vacation" 和第 38 篇 "My Personal Experience of Learning..." 互相套用。

50 Library

你會到圖書館看書嗎？請以圖書館為題寫一篇短文，第一段說明你如何看待圖書館這個場所，第二段闡述圖書館的功能或影響力。

I firmly believe that reading has a positive impact on people. Through reading, people not only gain knowledge but also develop a good habit. Therefore, a library can be defined as a place offering a wide range of [1]resources for reading and learning.

To me, a library is for people who enjoy reading in a quiet area. With an [2]extensive collection of books, a library provides quality services for people who can't [3]purchase such a large collection. For people who need books on [4]non-mainstream topics that no one can possibly have, a library can be of great help! [5]In addition to books, a library also provides easy [6]access to knowledge through various media such as CDs and DVDs. Thus, housing a variety of books and media, a library plays an important role in making a difference to the world. Since a library is [7]accessible to everyone, people can [8]enrich their lives through getting different resources at will. As a result, a library, with all the [9]advantages I [10]mentioned, can actually turn the world into a better place.

Total: 177 words

Vocabulary & Phrases in Use

1. **resource** n. 資源
2. **extensive** adj. 廣泛的
3. **purchase** v. 購買
4. **non-mainstream** adj. 非主流的
5. **in addition to...** phr. 除了…以外 (還)
6. **access to...** 取得…的機會
7. **accessible** adj. 可使用的
8. **enrich** v. 使豐富
9. **advantage** n. 好處，優點
10. **mention** v. 提到

Writing Tips

1. 本文主要著重於表達自我意見。 先以主題句 (topic sentence) 提出自己的立場 I firmly believe that...，敘述閱讀的重要性及圖書館的功能， 接著舉例來支持論點 (supporting details) ， 文章結尾以 a library...can actually turn the world into a better place. 總結對圖書館的看法，並呼應開頭的主題句，這樣的寫法在寫作時比較不易離題。

2. 本文常見用法有 a wide range of (各式各樣的) 、 provide sth for sb (為某人提供某物) 和 play an important role in... (在…扮演重要的角色) ， 還有關係代名詞 (...people who...) 和分詞用法 (housing..., a library...)。

51 The Subject I Like Best in School (History)

你最喜歡的科目是哪一科？請寫一篇英文作文，文分兩段，第一段說明你最喜歡的科目，以及喜歡該科的原因，第二段則分享你的學習心得。(本篇以文科為例)

　　Of all the subjects, I like history best because it is [1]fascinating to know about the past. History tells me lots of interesting stories of the past. Therefore, I find it more [2]appealing than science, including math, [3]physics, [4]biology, and [5]chemistry. At school, I always have so much fun studying history because it is just like reading a [6]serial story for pleasure and [7]relaxation or traveling back to the past.

　　Studying history can [8]benefit us. We can better understand the present and [9]predict the future by [10]analyzing the history, which tells us how things started and ended. From history, we can learn about the historic events and the origins of [11]civilizations. Hence, we may prevent ourselves from falling into the same trap, as others did before. All in all, history is the subject I like best in school.

Total: 138 words

Vocabulary & Phrases in Use

1. **fascinating** adj. 極有趣的
2. **appealing** adj. 有吸引力的
3. **physics** n. 物理學
4. **biology** n. 生物學
5. **chemistry** n. 化學
6. **serial** adj. 連載的
7. **relaxation** n. 放鬆
8. **benefit** v. 對…有益
9. **predict** v. 預料
10. **analyze** v. 分析，仔細研究
11. **civilization** n. 文明

Writing Tips

1. 本文分為兩段，主要內容分成：(1)最喜歡的科目。(2)說明學習的心得。在第一段講明要介紹的科目，並簡要介紹為什麼喜歡這個科目，第二段敘述學習的心得。

2. 本文常見用法有 analyze sth (分析某事)、historic event (重大歷史事件) 和 the origin of sth (某事的起源)，還有關係代名詞 (...history, which tells us...)。

52 The Subject I Like Best in School (Chemistry)

你最喜歡的科目是哪一科？請寫一篇英文作文，文分兩段，第一段說明你最喜歡的科目，以及喜歡該科的原因，第二段則分享你的學習心得。(本篇以理科為例)

The subject I like best in school is chemistry because it is a really cool subject and I [1]am good at it. My chemistry teacher is Mr. Chen, who always makes the class [2]enjoyable. Under his [3]guidance, we do a lot of interesting [4]experiments. Throughout the last [5]semester, we spent almost half of the time in the [6]lab. For me, all the experiments we have done are so valuable and so much fun.

Chemistry [7]plays a big part in our [8]daily lives. It is everywhere in the world around us. It is in the food we eat, water we drink, clothes we wear, [9]cleaners we use, and medicines we take. Studying chemistry is quite useful because it is the kind of knowledge that not just stays in books, but can be [10]put into practice. All in all, chemistry is my favorite subject, and I would like to major in chemistry in college in the future.

Total: 155 words

Vocabulary & Phrases in Use

1. **be good at...** 擅長⋯
2. **enjoyable** adj. 令人愉快的
3. **guidance** n. 指導
4. **experiment** n. 實驗
5. **semester** n. 學期
6. **lab** n. 實驗室
7. **play a part in...** phr.
   參與⋯，在⋯中起作用
8. **daily life** n. 日常生活
9. **cleaner** n. 清潔劑
10. **put...into practice** phr.
    將⋯付諸實行

Writing Tips

1. 本文的結構同第 51 篇 "The Subject I Like Best in School (History)"，分為兩段：(1)最喜歡的科目。(2)說明學習的心得。在第一段講明要介紹的科目，並簡要介紹為什麼喜歡這個科目，第二段敘述學習的心得。

2. 本文常見用法有 under one's guidance (在某人的指導下)、throughout... (在整個⋯期間)、daily life (日常生活)、put...into practice (將⋯付諸實行) 和 major in (主修)，可在寫作時多加運用。

53 A Rainy Day

每個人在不同的情況下對雨可能有不同的感受。請寫一篇英文作文，文分兩段，第一段敘述你在某個下雨天的實際經歷或看到的景象，第二段則據此描述你對雨的感覺。

One sweltering hot afternoon, I went to the library with my friend, Frank, to study for our upcoming entrance exams. However, as we were leaving the library, the rain was ¹pouring ²like crazy! I was very worried at that time because I didn't bring my umbrella with me. Fortunately, Frank brought his umbrella and walked me home, though his home was in a different direction from mine. On my way home, I saw many people on the street helplessly waiting for the rain to stop. At that moment, I felt warm and ³relieved because I had a friend who ⁴was willing to help me when I was in need. Even though it was so late that night, he still insisted on walking me home on such a rainy day.

After that day, whenever it rains, I ⁵recall Frank and our happy memories together. ⁶Apart from that, I also realize that I should always ⁷get prepared for everything ⁸in advance since things may happen ⁹unexpectedly anytime. Now I always ¹⁰make sure that I put an umbrella in my bag even if it is a sunny day!

Total: 185 words

1. **pour** v. (雨) 傾盆而下
2. **like crazy** phr. 瘋狂地
3. **relieved** adj. 放心的
4. **be willing to** 願意
5. **recall** v. 回想起
6. **apart from...** phr. 除了⋯之外

7. **get prepared for...**
   為⋯做準備
8. **in advance** phr. 事先
9. **unexpectedly** adv. 出乎意料地
10. **make sure** phr. 確認

Writing Tips

1. 本文以「下雨天」為主題，先敘述自己某個雨天的經歷，再描述對雨的感覺。敘述經歷以過去式時態為主，但是描述個人感覺屬於事實的陳述，所以用現在式時態。

2. 本文常見用法有 bring sth with sb (某人隨身攜帶某物) 和 be willing to (願意)，以及介系詞片語 apart from... (除了⋯之外)，可在寫作時多加運用。

3. 本文運用 bring one's umbrella with sb、be pouring like crazy 描述下雨天的情境，可在類似情境的文章中多加運用。

4. 本文的故事情節也可套用在描述友誼、好朋友和令人印象最深刻的一件事等類似情境的文章中。

54 When I'm in a Bad Mood

請以自己的經驗為例寫一篇短文，文分兩段，第一段敘述當你感到不快樂或情緒低落時，你最常用哪一種方法幫自己度過低潮，第二段則說明這個方法何以有效。

When I'm in a bad mood, I always read a novel that helps me ^{1}get through the unhappy times. Due to the heavy workload at school, I barely have free time to do any ^{2}outside reading. Still, whenever I feel upset, the first thing that I want to do is to pick up a novel and ^{3}bury myself in it.

By reading a novel, I can ^{4}escape from ^{5}reality and escape to a different world where my worries seem to ^{6}temporarily go away. What's more, a novel can even inspire me to find ways to solve my problems in life. After reading a novel for a few hours, I can quickly ^{7}restore my ^{8}confidence and ^{9}boost my energy. It is like traveling to a different world without leaving home. Reading a novel can really help me ^{10}cope with unhappiness and stress.

Total: 141 words

1. **get through** phr. 熬過
2. **outside reading** n. 課外閱讀
3. **bury oneself in...** phr. 專心投入…
4. **escape from** 逃離
5. **reality** n. 現實

6. **temporarily** adv. 暫時地
7. **restore** v. 恢復
8. **confidence** n. 信心
9. **boost** v. 提振
10. **cope with** phr. 應付

Writing Tips

1. 本文以 When I'm in a bad mood 為開頭，分為兩段，主要內容分成：(1)自身情緒低落時用哪一種方法度過低潮。(2)說明這個方法何以有效。

2. 本文常見用法有 in a bad mood (心情不好)、heavy workload (沉重的工作量) 和 go away (消失)，以及慣用語 what's more (而且)，可在寫作時多加運用。

3. 本文部分內容可套用在描述嗜好或最喜歡的休閒活動等類似情境的文章中。

55 How Can We Manage Our Time Efficiently?

你如何管理時間？你知道哪些有助於管理時間的方法嗎？請寫一篇短文論述管理時間的方法。文分兩段，第一段的第一句必須是 Managing time is very important. ，第二段的第一句必須是 Now, I have a new plan for using my time efficiently. 。

Managing time is very important. When I was in my [1]freshman year of senior high school, I had great difficulty managing my time. I had to deal with [2]a bunch of different subjects at school. In addition, I went to the [3]cram school twice a week. Sometimes, I also had to take part in some [4]extracurricular activities after school. How I wished that I had forty-eight hours a day!

Now, I have a new plan for using my time [5]efficiently. First, I will make a list of [6]priorities that I have to do. The most urgent thing should be [7]handled immediately. Second, I should pay attention in class all the time, so I don't have to spend a lot of time [8]reviewing at home. By doing so, I can not only make [9]progress in my studies, but also [10]make the time to enjoy a variety of extracurricular activities. To sum up, if I can use my time more wisely, I firmly believe that I can lead a [11]fulfilled life.

Total: 169 words

1. **freshman** n. 一年級新生
2. **a bunch of** 一堆
3. **cram school** n. 補習班
4. **extracurricular activity** n. 課外活動
5. **efficiently** adv. 有效率地
6. **priority** n. 優先事項
7. **handle** v. 處理
8. **review** v. 複習
9. **progress** n. 進步
10. **make (the) time...** phr. 騰出時間…
11. **fulfilled** adj. 滿足的

Writing Tips

1. 本文分為兩段，第一段敘述自己的經驗，藉以闡述主題句 Managing time is very important.，第二段則說明有助於管理時間的方法。

2. 本文運用 make a list of priorities、make (the) time...、use my time more wisely 來敘述如何善用時間，可套用在類似情境的文章中。

3. 本文常見用法有 make a list of priorities (列出優先事項)、not only...but also... (不僅…而且…)、firmly believe (堅信) 和 lead a...life (過…的生活)，可在寫作時多加運用。

56 My Plan After High School

下面有兩個問題，和你的未來計畫有關，每個問題請用大約 70 個單詞回答。

(1) Why do you want to enter college?

(2) What will you do if you don't go to college?

(1) I want to enter college for the following reasons. First, I hope to explore my interests and find out what I really want to do in the future. Second, I desire to [1]acquire more [2]specialized knowledge that will make me [3]competitive in the [4]job market. Last but not least, I also look forward to broadening my horizons by [5]making friends from different [6]backgrounds. Friendships are as important as knowledge from the books.

Total: 72 words

(2) If I don't go to college, I will take a [7]gap year to explore myself. During my gap year, I will go to Australia for a year's [8]working holiday and also [9]go backpacking around the country. In that way, I will not only sharpen my English skills but also [10]earn some money without relying on my parents. More importantly, I will learn how to be more independent. Then, I will decide my next step in life.

Total: 76 words

Vocabulary & Phrases in Use

1. **acquire** v. 獲得
2. **specialized** adj. 專業的
3. **competitive** adj. 有競爭力的
4. **job market** n. 就業市場
5. **make friends** phr. 交朋友

6. **background** n. 背景
7. **gap year** n. 空檔年
8. **working holiday** n. 打工渡假
9. **go backpacking** 背包旅行
10. **earn** v. 賺 (錢)

Writing Tips

1. 本文依提示分別回答兩個問題：(1)想進大學的原因；(2)如果不上大學的話，要做什麼？主要內容為(1)：解釋說明原因，時態為現在式。(2)：敘述未來計畫，時態為未來式。

2. 回答時可把主要的問句改為一般直述句當作回答的開頭，像是 I want to enter college... 以及 If I don't go to college...。此外，列點式的寫法通常最為清楚，可在第一句回答問題後，以分項列點的方式說明理由。

3. 本文常見用法有 look forward to (盼望)、broaden one's horizons (拓展某人的視野) 和 rely on (依靠)，還有關係代名詞 (...knowledge that will make...) 和條件句 (If I don't go to college, I will...)，可在類似情境的文章中多加運用。

119

57 A Shopping Experience

人們有各種不同的理由去逛街購物，相信你也有上街購物的經驗。請寫一篇英文作文，文分兩段，第一段說明你去購買的物品及理由，第二段敘述購物的經過，包括買回家後是否滿意等。

Last weekend, my sister and I went out to pick a [1]Mother's Day present for Mom. We first went to a big [2]department store by bus, but we couldn't find anything [3]suitable. Then, we went to a local [4]clothing store next to it. The store was small but [5]cozy. [6]The latest fashions hung all over the walls, and the clothes were of [7]good quality. Additionally, everything was at a special [8]discount for Mother's Day.

The clerk came to help us with a lovely smile. After knowing our reason for shopping, the clerk gave us some advice. Therefore, we chose a colorful dress with a floral design. This beautiful dress made a perfect gift! On seeing the gift, our mom [9]couldn't take her eyes off it. She loved it so much and said she would wear it the next day. Thanks to the [10]salesperson's advice, it was really a pleasant shopping experience.

Total: 151 words

Vocabulary & Phrases in Use

1. **Mother's Day present** n.
   母親節禮物

2. **department store** n. 百貨公司

3. **suitable** adj. 合適的

4. **clothing store** n. 服飾店

5. **cozy** adj. 舒適的

6. **the latest fashion** n.
   最新流行的款式

7. **good quality** n. 好品質

8. **discount** n. 折扣

9. **can't take one's eyes off...**
   phr. 目不轉睛地盯著…

10. **salesperson** n. 銷售人員

Writing Tips

1. 本文分為兩段，主要內容分成：(1)購物的原因及購買的物品。(2)購物的經驗與感想。主要時態為過去式。

2. 本文常見用法有 additionally (此外)、at a discount (打折)、thanks to (幸好)。

3. 本文內容可套用在描述買禮物給朋友等類似情境的文章中。

58 Social Media

請以 "Social Media" 為題，寫一篇英文作文敘述社群媒體的好處和壞處。第一段寫社群媒體的好處，第二段寫社群媒體的壞處。

　　Social media can be beneficial. Social media can help us keep in touch with our friends and also broaden our horizons quickly. We can contact our friends and know about their [1]status updates. Moreover, we can get the latest news and an extensive amount of knowledge from social media. What's more, social media can provide [2]entertainment for us. We can watch all kinds of short clips to relieve our tension.

　　However, social media can be [3]potentially [4]harmful to us. Unknowing users can [5]unconsciously [6]fall victim to it. Some social media platforms are full of sex, [7]violence, or [8]rumors that are spread repeatedly [9]over and over again. Furthermore, we barely have our own [10]privacy while using social media. What's worse, cases of [11]cyberbullying are increasing on the Internet. Any of us could be cyberbullied and deeply hurt. Therefore, we should be very careful when using social media.

Total: 146 words

Vocabulary & Phrases in Use

1. **status update** n. 近況
2. **entertainment** n. 娛樂
3. **potentially** adv. 潛在地
4. **harmful** adj. 有害的
5. **unconsciously** adv.
   不知不覺地
6. **fall victim to...** phr. 為…所害

7. **violence** n. 暴力
8. **rumor** n. 謠言
9. **over and over again** phr.
   一再地
10. **privacy** n. 隱私
11. **cyberbullying** n. 網路霸凌

Writing Tips

1. 本文為論說文，主要說明：⑴社群媒體的好處。⑵社群媒體的壞處。全文使用時態為現在式，並舉例支持所敘述的論點。

2. 本文常見用法有 keep in touch with sb (與某人保持聯繫)、broaden one's horizons (拓展某人的視野)、 be full of (充滿) 和 over and over again (一再地)，並適時運用轉折語，讓文章更流暢，例如：moreover 和 however。

3. 本文內容可套用在討論網路或使用網路等類似情境的文章中。

59 Ups and Downs

人的一生中有順境也有逆境，你有過在逆境中得到貴人幫助的經驗嗎？請寫一篇英文作文，文分兩段，第一段敘述你個人曾經遭遇的困境，第二段說明你如何解決問題，進而走出困境的過程。

I used to be a happy student and was good at all ¹academic subjects from ²elementary school to junior high school. However, when I was in senior high school, I felt upset due to the ³loss of my dear ⁴grandparents, who had been raising me since I was born. I started to ⁵skip class and began to spend a lot of time playing online games at a ⁶cybercafé near my home. As a result, I became more and more ⁷isolated from my family and friends.

Fortunately, next to the cybercafé, I met a noodle stand owner, Oliver. One day, when I was having a bowl of noodles, he told me that he had a son of my age. On seeing me, he was worried about me and shared his life experience with me. I was interested in listening to his stories and ⁸had a good time talking to him. He encouraged me to go back to school to study hard. In this way, I could make my late grandparents proud. After all those conversations, I felt ⁹motivated and started studying hard for my ¹⁰loved ones. Thanks to his encouragement, I have become happier, and I know my grandparents would be happy for me.

Total: 203 words

1. **academic subject** n. 學科
2. **elementary school** n. 小學
3. **loss** n. 逝世
4. **grandparents** n. (外) 祖父母
5. **skip class** 蹺課
6. **cybercafé** n. 網咖
7. **isolated** adj. 疏遠的
8. **have a good time**
   有愉快的時光
9. **motivated** adj. 受到激勵的
10. **loved one** n. 親人

Writing Tips

1. 本文分為兩段，主要內容分成：(1)個人遭遇困境的經驗。(2)突破困境的方法和過程。在敘述個人過去經驗時使用過去式時態。

2. 本文常見用法有 be good at (擅長)、on V-ing (一⋯就⋯) 和 be interested in... (對⋯感興趣)，並適時運用轉折語，讓文章更流暢，例如：as a result。

3. 本文內容可套用在敘述親友如何走出低潮等類似情境的文章中。

⑩ An Unforgettable Teacher

請寫一篇英文作文談談最令你難忘的老師，文分兩段，第一段描述該老師的特徵及個性，第二段說明令你難忘的理由。

Ms. Chang is the most unforgettable teacher that I've ever had in senior high school. She was of the same height as my mom, and her hair was long and ¹curly. She looked serious when she wore a pair of ²black-rimmed glasses, but her teaching style was so interesting and funny. Furthermore, she always taught her students with a smile. Her class was ³well-organized and full of laughs. However, she was also quite ⁴strict with us when we ⁵misbehaved.

She has a great ⁶impact on my life. I used to be ⁷far behind the rest of the class in all the subjects. She ⁸guided me patiently and told me to concentrate on my studies. Besides, she lent me many interesting books to help me develop a habit of reading and learn to read for enjoyment. She also asked my teachers from other subjects to pay special attention to me and helped me out when I had difficulties. ⁹Following Ms. Chang's advice, I tried to do my best in the studies and did improve a lot. I feel so lucky to be her student! I will always remember her ¹⁰warmness and patience.

Total: 191 words

Vocabulary & Phrases in Use

1. **curly** adj. 捲曲的
2. **black-rimmed glasses** n. 黑框眼鏡
3. **well-organized** adj. 井然有序的
4. **strict** adj. 嚴格的
5. **misbehave** v. 行為不良

6. **impact** n. 影響 (力)
7. **far behind** 遠遠落後於
8. **guide** v. 指導
9. **follow one's advice** 遵照某人的忠告
10. **warmness** n. 溫暖

Writing Tips

1. 本文分為兩段，主要內容分成：(1)難忘的老師之特徵及個性。(2)難忘的理由。敘述個人過去經驗時使用過去式時態。

2. 本文常見用法有 have an impact on... (對…有影響)、used to (過去曾經) 和 develop a habit of... (養成…習慣)，還有分詞用法 (Following Ms. Chang's advice, I tried...)。

3. 本文部分內容可用於描述求學時期最喜歡的老師或敘述印象最深刻的一件事等；其中第二段內容 ...develop a habit of reading and learn to read for enjoyment 與第 39 篇 "I Want to Be..." 文章用法相同，可在類似情境的文章中多加運用。

61 An Act of Kindness

溫情滿人間，請寫一篇英文作文敘述自己幫助他人的一次經驗。
文分兩段，第一段敘述事件發生的經過，第二段則說明後續發展
及感想。

Last weekend, I [1]left home for [2]the suburbs to visit my aunt.
That was my first time to take the train all by myself. Everything
went well until one thing happened. As soon as I [3]was about to [4]step
out of the train, I found someone's [5]purse left on the seat. [6]Without
a second thought, I kept it until I got off the train and [7]immediately
handed it to [8]the lost-and-found. When the [9]station staff opened the
purse, money, an ID card, and a train ticket were all in there! I could
imagine how worried the owner of the purse would be.

At that moment, an old lady headed toward the information
desk to ask about her purse. According to the description, the purse I
found was hers. The lady was so happy to find it because there were
so many valuable things inside. She felt so grateful for my act of
[10]kindness and thanked me many times. Later, my aunt picked me
up, and I told her what had happened. She praised me for my
kindness, and I felt so glad to help others in need.

Total: 187 words

Vocabulary & Phrases in Use

1. **leave...for...** 離開…前往…
2. **the suburbs** n. 郊區
3. **be about to + V** phr.
   正要做…
4. **step out of** 步出
5. **purse** n. 錢包
6. **without a second thought**
   phr. 毫不猶豫
7. **immediately** adv. 立刻
8. **the lost-and-found** n.
   失物招領處
9. **station staff** n. 站務員
10. **kindness** n. 仁慈

Writing Tips

1. 本文依提示敘述自己幫助他人的一次經驗，使用過去式時態，內容
   著重於：(1)主要發生的事件。(2)事件的後續及感想。

2. 本文常見用法有 be about to + V (正要做…)、pick sb up (開車接某
   人) 和 praise sb for sth (因為某事而稱讚某人)，可在寫作時多加運
   用。

3. 本文第一段的最後一句 I could imagine how... (我能想像…) 可用
   在描述某人想像出的情景，可在類似情境的文章中多加運用。

4. 本文部分內容可套用在敘述物品遺失的經驗或受他人幫忙找到遺
   失物等類似情境的文章中， 例如第 19 篇 "Honesty Is the Best
   Policy"。

62 Life with a Smartphone

現代人在日常生活裡越來越依賴智慧型手機，請寫一篇英文作文，分成兩段，第一段說明智慧型手機對我們生活的重要性，第二段描述你在日常生活中如何運用智慧型手機。

With the rapid ¹development of ²mobile ³communications technology ⁴in recent years, smartphones have been widely accepted and become necessities in our lives. Smartphones are able to perform many different functions. We use them to ⁵surf the Internet, make phone calls, take photos, send and receive emails, listen to music, and play games. We can even use them to pay the ⁶bills or ⁷run a business. In short, smartphones have changed the way we work, live, and play!

When it comes to life with a smartphone, I believe that it is more convenient than the one without a smartphone. It provides a ⁸means of quick communication and instant access to the Internet. With a smartphone, I can call a friend, send a text message to a friend, and write an email. Furthermore, by posting a public message on the social media platforms, I can record an ⁹incident and share it with hundreds of people ¹⁰within seconds. Indeed, a smartphone is ¹¹essential to my daily life.

Total: 164 words

Vocabulary & Phrases in Use

1. **development** n. 發展
2. **mobile** adj. 行動的
3. **communications** n. 通訊
4. **in recent years** 近年
5. **surf the Internet** 上網
6. **bill** n. 帳單

7. **run a business** 經營商店
8. **means** n. 方法
9. **incident** n. 事件
10. **within seconds** 一下子
11. **essential** adj. 極其重要的

Writing Tips

1. 本文分為兩段，主要內容分成：⑴智慧型手機對我們生活的重要性。⑵描述自己在日常生活中如何運用智慧型手機。

2. 本文常見用法有 run a business (經營商店)、when it comes to... (談到⋯)、access to... (使用⋯的途徑) 和 daily life (日常生活)。

3. 本文內容可套用在討論智慧型手機之重要性等類似情境的文章中。

63 Life Without a Smartphone

現代人在日常生活裡似乎離不開智慧型手機，請以 "Life Without a Smartphone" 為主題寫一篇英文作文，文章分成兩段，第一段說明智慧型手機對我們生活的重要性，第二段描述自己如何看待如果沒有智慧型手機的生活。

    With the rapid development of mobile communications technology in recent years, smartphones have been widely accepted and become necessities in our lives. Without smartphones, it will be very inconvenient to do many different things. We will not be able to surf the Internet, make phone calls, take photos, send and receive emails, use instant messaging, or play games easily and quickly almost everywhere. In short, life will be not so convenient if there are no smartphones.

    What if I lived without a smartphone in today's world? At first, I think it would bring me lots of [1]inconvenience. However, from a different [2]point of view, I thought of some merits. For example, I would not be always [3]anxiously checking my [4]notifications or [5]replying to my friends' messages [6]instantly. I would probably have a lot more face-to-face communication with my family and friends. I would not [7]stare at the phone while walking on the street. What's more, I would never have to pay for [8]Internet access. [9]To sum up, I would be [10]better off living without a smartphone.

Total: 176 words

Vocabulary & Phrases in Use

1. **inconvenience** n. 不便
2. **point of view** n. 想法
3. **anxiously** adv. 焦慮地
4. **notification** n. 通知
5. **reply** v. 回覆

6. **instantly** adv. 立即地
7. **stare at...** 注視，盯著⋯
8. **Internet access** n. 網際網路
9. **to sum up** phr. 總而言之
10. **better off** adj. 更幸福，更滿意

Writing Tips

1. 本文分為兩段，主要內容分成：(1)智慧型手機對我們生活的重要性。(2)描述自己如何看待如果沒有智慧型手機的生活。須注意如果在現實生活中有手機，那麼因為第二段文章內容與現在實際情況不同，要使用「與現在事實相反」的假設語氣。

2. 本文常見用法有 point of view (想法) 和 to sum up (總而言之)，以及假設語氣 (I would never...)，可在寫作時多加運用。

64 A Wonderful Person

日常生活中，總可發現出現在我們身邊的好人，也許是我們的親人、師長、朋友，或甚至只是在公車上給我們一塊錢幫我們補足車資的陌生人。請寫一篇英文作文描述你曾碰過的好人，文分兩段，第一段描述其人其行，第二段說明這位好人對你的影響。

Ms. Huang, my [1]geography teacher, is a wonderful person. She is patient and [2]exceptionally understanding. I used to be a shy and [3]sensitive person. Therefore, I had difficulty making friends. Whenever I talked to Ms. Huang, she always listened to me and [4]put herself in my shoes. She showed me how to [5]socialize with others in [6]proper ways. Furthermore, she also gave me some tips on how to start a conversation with people around me.

Her words always inspired me and made me feel [7]refreshed. As a result, I usually took her advice, and it really worked. One day, one of my friends told me that I have become a friendlier person to [8]get along with. I really appreciate Ms. Huang's help and cherish every moment of being her student. To me, she is a perfect example of a wonderful person who has [9]enlightened me [10]profoundly.

Total: 145 words

Vocabulary & Phrases in Use

1. **geography** n. 地理
2. **exceptionally** adv. 特別地
3. **sensitive** adj. 敏感的
4. **put oneself in one's shoes** phr. 設身處地為某人著想
5. **socialize** v. 交際
6. **proper** adj. 適當的
7. **refreshed** adj. 精神振作的
8. **get along with...** phr. 與…和睦相處
9. **enlighten** v. 啟發
10. **profoundly** adv. 深刻地

Writing Tips

1. 本文依提示，描述一位好人的特質、事蹟與影響。必須注意時態的變化，陳述一般事實或個人想法時，以現在式為主，描述過去經驗時，則以過去式為主。

2. 寫作時可適時運用副詞 (片語)，讓文章更流暢，例如：therefore 和 as a result。

3. 本文中的 patient 和 understanding 可以形容人有耐心和善解人意；另外，shy 和 sensitive 則可形容人害羞和敏感，這些描述某人個性的用法可在其他類似情境的文章中多加運用。

4. 本文內容可放在敘述求學時期最喜歡的老師或是令人印象最深刻的老師等類似情境的文章中，像是第 60 篇 "An Unforgettable Teacher" 文章。

65 My Favorite Spot in the World

人在苦惱的時候，常會找個地方靜下心來好好放鬆。請寫一篇英文作文，描述能讓你身心寧靜或放鬆的地方，第一段描述在什麼情況下，你會到這個地方讓自己靜心放鬆，第二段則說明該處的特別之處以及你喜歡它的原因。

[1]It goes without saying that everyone has his or her own favorite spot to go to whenever he or she feels upset. My favorite spot in the world is a bench under the trees by the playground in my school. Whenever I'm in a bad mood because of a low grade or a [2]quarrel with a friend, I go there to calm myself down.

Sitting under the trees and looking at other students [3]jogging around the running [4]tracks, I turn my attention to them. At that time, I forget about those unpleasant things. When I see a smiling face, I smile back. When I see someone [5]frowning, I wonder if that person needs some help. Sometimes, I just stare at a [6]cloudless sky and relax myself. After a while, I stop feeling down as the sky is so big that seems to have absorbed all of my [7]sadness. Though it is just a corner of the school, that [8]tiny world has the [9]magical power to [10]clear my mind and make me feel better.

Total: 173 words

1. **it goes without saying that...** phr. …不言而喻
2. **quarrel** n. 爭吵
3. **jog** v. 慢跑
4. **track** n. 跑道
5. **frown** v. 皺眉
6. **cloudless** adj. 晴朗無雲的
7. **sadness** n. 悲傷
8. **tiny** adj. 微小的
9. **magical** adj. 有魔力的
10. **clear one's mind**
    使某人頭腦清醒

Writing Tips

1. 此類陳述個人想法或選擇的文章以現在式時態為主。本文開頭先描述讓自己靜心放鬆的地方，並說明在何種情況下會去這個地方，進而敘述這個地方的特別之處以及讓自己喜歡的原因。本文內容可套用在類似情境的文章中，例如第 54 篇 "When I'm in a Bad Mood"。

2. 本文常見用法有 it goes without saying that... (…不言而喻)、in a bad mood (心情不好) 和 calm...down (使…平靜下來)，還有分詞 (Sitting under the trees..., I turn...)，並適時運用連接詞，讓文章更流暢，例如：whenever 和 though。

66 A Special Day to Remember

請寫一篇英文作文敘述你所記得的一個特別的日子。文分兩段，第一段描述這個日子發生什麼事，第二段則說明這個日子為什麼會特別令你懷念。

I have a cousin, Ashley, who is a [1]social worker. Two months ago, she took me to an [2]orphanage. We spent the whole day there playing with the kids and helping them with their homework. At first, they were a little [3]timid and [4]hesitated over [5]getting close to me. However, after I showed my [6]friendliness, some of the kids [7]gathered around me and shared lots of things with me. I [8]had a great time with them that day.

After [9]a long day, when I was about to leave there, one little girl even came to give me a lovely picture that she had drawn. At that time, I was deeply [10]moved. After getting along with the kids in the orphanage that day, I knew I could also help others in need. That was really a special day for me to remember.

Total: 141 words

1. **social worker** n. 社工
2. **orphanage** n. 孤兒院
3. **timid** adj. 羞怯的
4. **hesitate** v. 猶豫
5. **get close to...** 接近…
6. **friendliness** n. 友善
7. **gather** v. 聚集
8. **have a great time with...** phr. 與…過得愉快
9. **a long day** 漫長的一天
10. **moved** adj. 感動的

Writing Tips

1. 本文依提示敘述一個特別的日子，並闡述其令人懷念的理由，且文章結尾用 That was really a special day for me to remember. 來強調這個難忘的特別日子。

2. 本文常見用法有 help sb with... (幫助某人…)、have a great time with... (與…過得愉快) 和 get along with... (與…和睦相處)，可在寫作時多加運用。

3. 本文內容可套用在描述難忘的經驗等類似情境的文章中。

67 A Great Achievement

雖然人生難免碰到諸多挫折，可是每個人的一生當中也會有足以令人自豪的表現。請寫一篇英文作文描述一件你人生中最得意的事，以及對這件事的感想。

When I was in my second grade of senior high school, I was [1]appointed by my English teacher to [2]take part in an English speech [3]contest held by the school. At first, I was very nervous since I spent little time practicing speaking English. Furthermore, I didn't think I had the ability to [4]compete in such a contest. Nevertheless, with encouragement from my English teacher, I made up my mind to [5]go all out for it. Before the speech contest, I practiced very hard and [6]discussed how to make my performance better with my English teacher every day. When the contest finally [7]took place, I tried my best to [8]give a speech in front of the [9]judges and got second prize! I was so happy with the result and proud of myself. From the experience, I realized that [10]practice makes perfect.

Total: 141 words

Vocabulary & Phrases in Use

1. **appoint** v. 指派
2. **take part in** phr. 參加
3. **contest** n. 比賽
4. **compete** v. 競爭
5. **go all out for sth** phr.
   全力以赴做某事

6. **discuss** v. 討論
7. **take place** phr. 舉行，舉辦
8. **give a speech** 演講
9. **judge** n. 評審
10. **practice makes perfect** phr.
    熟能生巧

Writing Tips

1. 使用過去式時態敘述自己的一項成就，並進而闡述這項成就發生的背景及過程，以及事後對個人的影響。

2. 本文常見用法有 take part in (參加)、make up one's mind to... (下定決心做…) 和 be happy with... (對…滿意的)，並適時運用轉折語，讓文章更流暢，例如：furthermore 和 nevertheless。

3. 本文部分內容可套用在敘述求學時期印象最深刻的一件事或是感謝老師的一則故事等類似情境的文章中。

68 My Best...Class Ever

請以 "My Best...Class Ever" 為題寫一篇英文作文，文分兩段，第一段描述你上過最充實且令你印象深刻的一堂課，第二段則說明你喜歡這堂課的原因。

My best math class ever was when I was in my freshman year of junior high school. I met a math teacher, Mr. Mitchell, who not only taught us math but also shared with us how to ¹work through the ²problem-solving ³tasks in our daily lives. He kept on ⁴emphasizing the ⁵importance of ⁶independent thinking. Furthermore, he also recommended many interesting books to us in order to help us develop a habit of reading and learn to read for enjoyment. He said that reading can improve our ⁷logical thinking and help us work out math problems.

One day, he showed us a short clip at the beginning of the class and then asked us to do some brainstorming. Under his guidance, we learned how to ⁸accurately ⁹calculate how much money we have to pay, how to think logically, and how to ¹⁰solve the problems. In that class, with his interesting teaching style and encouragement, I found math so enjoyable, and I could also put my knowledge into practice in life. It was the best math class I've ever had.

Total: 179 words

Vocabulary & Phrases in Use

1. **work through** phr. 解決 (問題)
2. **problem-solving** adj.
   解決問題的
3. **task** n. 任務
4. **emphasize** v. 強調
5. **importance** n. 重要性
6. **independent thinking** n.
   獨立思考
7. **logical** adj. 合乎邏輯的
8. **accurately** adv. 精確地
9. **calculate** v. 計算
10. **solve** v. 解決

Writing Tips

1. 本文開頭先點出要描述的對象，再敘述關於這堂課的內容，以及為什麼喜歡它的緣故，並提供鮮明的例子來突顯主題。

2. 本文常見用法有 develop a habit of... (養成…習慣)、under one's guidance (在某人的指導下) 和 put...into practice (將…付諸實行)，可在寫作時多加運用。

3. 本文部分內容可套用在描述求學時期最喜歡的科目或老師或是印象最深刻的一件事等類似情境的文章中，例如第 51 篇 "The Subject I Like Best in School (History)" 或第 60 篇 "An Unforgettable Teacher"。

⑥ One Thing to Be Done Before Graduation

高中生涯即將進入尾聲，有沒有哪一件事情是你希望在高中畢業前一定要完成的？請寫一篇英文作文，第一段說明這件事是什麼，以及你為什麼希望在高中畢業前一定要完成這件事，第二段說明你將如何完成這件事。

I have seven good friends in senior high school, and we are not just friends but more like family. I hope that someday we can go to Kenting together to enjoy the ¹bright sunshine and the blue ocean. But now, we are in the last semester of high school, and we haven't found the time to go yet. After several months, we will go to different colleges. So, I hope we can ²realize the dream before ³graduating from high school.

To achieve the goal, I have to ⁴make a ⁵feasible plan. First, I have to find some time when all of us are free. Second, I have to ⁶map out a plan for the ⁷transportation to Kenting. Last but not least, safe and clean ⁸accommodations must be ⁹reserved in advance. In that way, we can be ¹⁰in a good mood in Kenting together.

Total: 143 words

Vocabulary & Phrases in Use

1. **bright sunshine** n.
   明媚的陽光
2. **realize** v. 實現
3. **graduate** v. 畢業
4. **make a plan** 訂計畫
5. **feasible** adj. 可行的
6. **map out** phr. 詳細規畫
7. **transportation** n. 交通工具
8. **accommodations** n. 住宿
9. **reserve** v. 預約
10. **in a good mood** phr. 有好心情

Writing Tips

1. 本文依提示在第一段說明要完成什麼事，並解釋原因為何，且在第二段說明如何達成這件事。注意全文應以高中畢業前一定要完成的「一件事」為主，避免將一些細微末節的事情也寫進去，以免模糊了焦點。

2. 本文常見用法有 realize the dream (實現夢想) 和 in advance (事先)，可在寫作時多加運用。

3. 本文內容可套用在如何計畫畢業旅行或暑假旅行等類似情境的文章中。

⑩ The Role I Played Best in My Life

每個人在一生中往往同時扮演著很多角色，例如你是高中生，同時是你父母的孩子，也是同儕的朋友。請寫一篇英文作文，文分兩段，第一段敘述你覺得自己扮演得最好的一個角色，第二段說明為何你會這麼認為。

As a 17-year-old person, I play different roles in different places. I'm a child to my parents, a student to my teachers, and a friend to my ¹peers. I try my best to play all the roles in my life, but among these roles, I'm most successful in being a good friend. To me, friends are precious. I'm proud that I'm a ²humorous and ³trustworthy ⁴soulmate to my friends.

⁵In my friends' eyes, I'm just like their family because I'm always willing to help them when they are in need. I ⁶keep them company when they feel lonely, and I tell them some jokes when they feel down. Furthermore, I give them advice when they ⁷are in trouble. ⁸Most of all, I'm always a ⁹reliable and ¹⁰thoughtful person when my friends need my help. Thus, among all the roles that I play in life, I believe that I play the friend's role best. I'm also happy that I have so many good friends in return.

Total: 165 words

Vocabulary & Phrases in Use

1. **peer** n. 同儕
2. **humorous** adj. 幽默的
3. **trustworthy** adj. 值得信賴的
4. **soulmate** n. 知己
5. **in one's eyes** phr.
   在某人眼裡，在某人看來
6. **keep sb company** phr.
   陪伴某人
7. **be in trouble** phr. 陷入困境
8. **most of all** phr. 最重要的是
9. **reliable** adj. 可信賴的
10. **thoughtful** adj. 體貼的

Writing Tips

1. 本文依提示敘述一個自己扮演起來最得心應手的角色，並舉例說明理由。

2. 本文常見用法有 in one's eyes (在某人眼裡)、be willing to (願意) 和 in return (作為回報)，以及同位語 a child to my parents, a student to my teachers, and a friend to my peers (父母的孩子，老師的學生，同儕的朋友)，並適時運用轉折語，讓文章更流暢，例如：furthermore。

3. 本文有描述一個人個性正向的形容詞，例如：humorous 和 trustworthy，可在類似情境的文章中多加運用。

71 A Perfect Day

你曾經歷過美好的一天嗎?或是有想過美好的一天會是什麼樣子嗎?請寫一篇至少 120 個單詞的英文作文,描述你曾經歷過或是你心目中美好的一天,以及如何度過這天。

My perfect day began with a bright Sunday morning. I had a delicious breakfast that my parents prepared for me, and I felt ^{1}energetic. Then, I called my friends and played basketball in the park together. The ^{2}teamwork between my ^{3}teammates and me was so ^{4}remarkable that we scored ten points ^{5}in a row. At noon, one of my friends treated us to drinks in the ^{6}convenience store. In the afternoon, we chatted and had a good time together in a café. Later that evening, I went back home for dinner, and my father told us ^{7}numerous funny stories about him and his ^{8}colleagues during his two-week ^{9}business trip. That night, we enjoyed a great meal and then watched a movie on TV together. To me, a perfect day is a day I spend ^{10}quality time with my family and friends.

Total: 141 words

Vocabulary & Phrases in Use

1. **energetic** adj. 精力充沛的
2. **teamwork** n. 團隊合作
3. **teammate** n. 隊員
4. **remarkable** adj. 出色的
5. **in a row** phr. 連續地
6. **convenience store** n.
   便利商店
7. **numerous** adj. 許多的
8. **colleague** n. 同事
9. **business trip** n. 出差
10. **quality time** n.
    (與親友等共享的) 優質時光

Writing Tips

1. 個人心目中美好的一天可以是已發生過的事實；也可以是自己心目中的理想狀態，也就是還沒發生，但自己希望發生的事。如果是前者，全篇使用過去式；如果是後者，則以現在式為主，但可搭配運用 would 和 should 這類助動詞，例如：It should be a sunny day. 和 I would love to walk my dog for two hours in the park.。

2. 描述如何度過一天時，可運用時間副詞，例如：then、at noon、later，讓文章時序清楚、層次分明，但應慎選描述的重點，避免講述刷牙、洗臉、綁鞋帶等生活瑣事。

3. 本文常見用法有 begin with... (以…開始)，還有關係代名詞 (...breakfast that my parents...)。

4. 本文內容可套用在描述最值得紀念的一天等類似情境的文章中。

149

⑫ Packing for a Year Abroad

在忙碌的課業中，你曾想過打包行李，出國一年去親身體驗自己有興趣的事物嗎？請以 "Packing for a Year Abroad" 為題，寫一篇英文作文，文分兩段。第一段描述在此一年中，你會選擇什麼地點？第二段則說明你會在該地點進行什麼樣的活動？你會以什麼樣的態度來度過在異鄉的一年？

As a high school graduate, if I have the chance to live abroad for one year, I will spend half a year in the U.S. and another half in England in order to sharpen my English listening and speaking skills. This will enable me to experience the beauty and [1]cultural differences between these two [2]English-speaking countries.

During my stay in the U.S., I will apply for a homestay and visit some [3]world-famous spots there in New York, such as the [4]Statue of Liberty and [5]Times Square. As to my stay in England, I will work part-time so as to support myself [6]financially to visit the [7]major cities, such as London, Cambridge, and Oxford. In doing so, I will be not only a tourist, but also an [8]explorer. I will communicate with the local people in English and know more about these two countries [9]respectively. Also, I will learn to [10]take a [11]liberal and [12]humble attitude toward the customs there. To sum up, I believe I will get lots of wonderful experiences in both countries and have a colorful year. Most of all, my English will definitely improve a lot.

Total: 189 words

Vocabulary & Phrases in Use

1. **cultural difference** n.
   文化差異
2. **English-speaking** adj.
   說英語的
3. **world-famous spot** n.
   世界著名景點
4. **Statue of Liberty** n.
   自由女神像
5. **Times Square** n. 時代廣場
6. **financially** adv. 財務上地
7. **major** adj. 主要的
8. **explorer** n. 探險家
9. **respectively** adv. 各別地
10. **take a(n)...attitude** 持…態度
11. **liberal** adj. 開明的
12. **humble** adj. 謙虛的

Writing Tips

1. 本文依提示在第一段寫出自己想去的地點，並說明想去此地的理由，在第二段進一步描述如何在此地度過一年。

2. 在敘述自己一年中的旅行計畫時，情境可不限於一個國家，可擴展成兩個國家，並描述這些國家吸引自己的旅遊景點和文化特色等，可使內容更豐富。

3. 本文常見用法有 sharpen one's English listening and speaking skills (精進某人的英語聽說技能) 和 take a(n)...attitude (持…態度)，還有假設語氣 (if...)，並善加運用時間副詞 (during my stay)，讓文章更清楚。

4. 本文部分內容可套用在描述未來想旅遊的國家、最喜歡的國家或計畫下一個旅遊景點等類似情境的文章中。

73 If I Had Magical Powers, I Would...

如果你具有魔法 (magical powers)，你最想做的改變是什麼？請寫一篇英文作文，文分兩段，第一段描述你最想用魔法改變什麼，第二段則說明理由。

If I had magical powers, I would use the power to control time. To be more [1]specific, I want to [2]extend each day so that I can [3]diversify my life every day.

Actually, my life is [4]consumed by school and cram school. Whenever I go back home at about ten at night, I still [5]can't go to sleep until I finish my homework and prepare for many quizzes for the next day. Thus, I don't have time to [6]develop other interests. With the power to control time, I would be [7]capable of lengthening a day to forty-eight hours. In this way, schoolwork would [8]no longer dominate my life. After the first half of the day, I would still have lots of time to do what I like, such as going to the gym and taking care of stray animals in the animal shelters. Although some people may worry whether forty-eight hours a day would [9]drag a student down, I'm [10]convinced that this is a balanced life I prefer.

Total: 168 words

Vocabulary & Phrases in Use

1. **specific** adj. 明確的	6. **develop** v. 發展，培養
2. **extend** v. 延長	7. **capable** adj. 有能力的
3. **diversify** v. 使多元化	8. **no longer** phr. 不再
4. **consume** v. 耗盡	9. **drag sb down** phr. 拖垮某人
5. **not...until...** phr. 直到…才…	10. **convinced** adj. 確信的

Writing Tips

1. 本文為說明文，第一段闡述個人想用魔法改變的事情，第二段則說明動機，最後再次強調自己想做的改變。

2. 本文常見用法有 not...until... (直到…才…) 、 be capable of... (能夠…) 和 I'm convinced that... (我確信…)，還有假設語氣 (if...)，並適時運用連接詞和副詞，讓文章更流暢，例如：whenever 和 thus。

⁊⁴ Making Up with...

人與人之間難免有誤會或爭執，請以此為主題寫一篇英文作文，文分兩段，第一段描述過去與他人發生誤會或爭吵的一次經驗，第二段舉例說明你解決的方式是和解 (make up) 或絕交 (break up)，以及最後的結果和感想。

I had an ¹unpleasant experience with my good friend, Alice. I had a lunch date with her one morning. However, I had to take my ²severely ill cat to the ³vet as well. Therefore, I was late for my date with Alice. Waiting for me for more than one hour, she went mad and didn't talk to me over a week.

When I called her to say sorry, she ⁴hung up the phone. I even tried to send her dozens of messages to make apologies, but there was no response. Feeling ⁵helpless, I had no choice but to ⁶turn to our ⁷mutual friend, Benjamin, for help. Although Benjamin and I were only ⁸nodding acquaintances, he ⁹spared no effort to ¹⁰persuade Alice to see me in person. After a long talk with Alice, she finally understood my ¹¹dilemma, and we ¹²made up with each other. From this experience, I learned that it would never be easy to make up with a friend after a fight, but where there's a will, there's a way.

Total: 173 words

Vocabulary & Phrases in Use

1. **unpleasant** adj. 不愉快的
2. **severely** adv. 嚴重地
3. **vet** n. 獸醫
4. **hang up** phr. 掛 (電話)
5. **helpless** adj. 無助的
6. **turn to sb for help**
   向某人尋求幫助
7. **mutual** adj. 共同的
8. **nodding acquaintance** n.
   點頭之交
9. **spare no effort to...** phr.
   不遺餘力去做…
10. **persuade** v. 說服
11. **dilemma** n. 兩難
12. **make up with sb** phr.
    和某人和好

Writing Tips

1. 本文依提示在第一段描寫自己和他人爭吵的經過，並在第二段描述個人採取的應對措施，接著再說明這樣做的結果，以及帶給自己什麼樣的感想。在描述過去發生的經驗時使用過去式時態。

2. 本文常見用法有 have no choice but to... (不得不…)、turn to sb for help (向某人尋求幫助)、in person (親自) 和 make up with sb (和某人和好)，還有分詞用法 (Waiting for me for more than one hour, she went... 和 Feeling helpless, I had...)，並適時運用轉折語 however、therefore、but，突顯出故事的轉折。

3. 本文內容可套用在描述學到的教訓或難忘的一件事等類似情境的文章中。

75 The Season I Like Best

請以 "The Season I Like Best" 為題 ， 寫一篇英文作文 ， 文分兩段，第一段敘述最喜歡的季節及理由，第二段描述該季節之景象或說明可從事的活動。

Personally, winter is my favorite season of the year. Unlike the hot weather in summer, the cold weather in winter ¹prompts me to be more ²self-motivated and hard-working. Interestingly, instead of ³curling up in bed, I do things more effectively during wintertime.

Moreover, winter brings people to ⁴engage in various activities together. Take the winter in Taiwan, for example. Restaurants ⁵are crowded with people to enjoy ⁶hot pots as the weather turns colder and colder. Taking ⁷hot springs is also an ⁸alternative among friends and families to take the chill off. Besides, one of the most important holidays of the year, Chinese New Year, falls in the winter season. Family members, regardless of long distance and busy schedules, celebrate the coming new year with a wonderful ⁹reunion dinner. Despite the low temperature, people actually feel a sense of warmth due to many activities and holidays that bring them together in winter. ¹⁰Briefly speaking, of the four seasons, I like winter most.

Total: 161 words

1. **prompt** v. 促使
2. **self-motivated** adj.
   自動自發的，積極的
3. **curl up in bed** 蜷曲在床上
4. **engage in** phr. 從事
5. **be crowded with...** 擠滿…

6. **hot pot** n. 火鍋
7. **hot spring** n. 溫泉
8. **alternative** n. 可供選擇的事物
9. **reunion** n. 團圓
10. **briefly speaking** 簡而言之

Writing Tips

1. 本文依提示在第一段描寫個人最喜歡某個季節的原因，第二段則透過舉例具體描述此季節的景象或在該季節裡的特別活動。

2. 本文主題為描述個人最喜歡的季節，所以不宜加入任何有關此季節的負面敘述，以免模糊焦點。

3. 本文常見用法有 engage in (從事)、various activities (各式各樣的活動) 和 regardless of (不管) 以及動名詞放在句首當主詞 (Taking hot springs is...)，並適時運用副詞和轉折語，讓文章更流暢，例如：personally、interestingly、moreover。

4. 本文部分內容可套用在描述寒假最喜歡的活動等類似情境的文章中。

76 The Most Important Values My Parents Have Taught Me

父母對子女教導及傳承許多價值觀，如獨立、誠實、心存感激、勤奮工作和尊師重道等。請以一個你認為最重要且影響你最大的價值觀來寫一篇英文作文，文分兩段，第一段說明此價值觀為何，第二段描述此價值觀在你成長經驗中所造成的影響。

¹Independence is the most important values which my parents have been teaching me repeatedly since my childhood. They taught me to be independent so that I could face the ²challenging world by myself instead of relying on other people's help all the time.

To put the ³principle of independence into practice, I have learned to count on myself since high school. On weekends and during the summer vacation, I work part-time so as not to burden my parents with financial stress. Therefore, I no longer depend on my parents for my ⁴tuition and ⁵living expenses. What's more, I'm independent enough to handle the ⁶frustrations and difficulties ⁷in terms of my studies and work without troubling my friends and ⁸beloved family. All in all, I thank my parents for teaching me the ⁹essence of independence, and I would cherish it as a ¹⁰philosophy of life.

Total: 144 words

1. **independence** n. 獨立
2. **challenging** adj. 有挑戰性的
3. **principle** n. 原則
4. **tuition** n. 學費
5. **living expenses** n. 生活開銷

6. **frustration** n. 挫折
7. **in terms of...** phr. 就…而言
8. **beloved** adj. 心愛的
9. **essence** n. 精髓
10. **philosophy of life** n. 人生哲學

Writing Tips

1. 本文依提示在第一段說明一個影響個人至深的價值觀，第二段舉例描述自己在生活中如何實踐此價值觀。此類文章適合在第一段就開宗明義寫出一項價值觀，然後進一步說明，而不是在文章中間才點出主旨。

2. 本文常見用法有 put...into practice (將…付諸實行)、no longer (不再) 和 thank sb for doing sth (感謝某人做某事)，還有關係代名詞 (Independence is the most important values which...)。

77 Learning in the Age of Technology

說到教學模式，有些學生喜歡教室中和老師面對面的教學情境，也有些學生偏好運用多媒體設備進行遠距學習。在這兩種學習方式中，你比較喜歡哪一種？請以此為主題寫一篇英文作文，文分兩段，第一段說明你的選擇與原因，第二段提出你做這個選擇的理由。

Some students learn better through [1]conventional ways that require them to go to school and have [2]face-to-face interaction with teachers. Other students prefer [3]distance learning with the help of [4]multimedia to obtain knowledge anytime and anywhere. From my [5]viewpoint, I prefer [6]attending school in person because I learn effectively in a classroom environment and gain more from interaction with my classmates.

In the first place, learning in a classroom enables me to understand the subjects better. That is, when I [7]encounter some problems in class, I can always ask teachers and [8]seek immediate help. Additionally, the interaction between me and my classmates is important as well. There is a proverb that goes, "Two heads are better than one." Studying alone, I'm usually [9]confined to certain perspectives. However, when I interact with classmates, I can [10]brainstorm and think of new ideas with them. For these reasons, I prefer attending school in person.

Total: 151 words

Vocabulary & Phrases in Use

1. **conventional** adj. 傳統的
2. **face-to-face** adj. 面對面的
3. **distance learning** n. 遠距教學
4. **multimedia** n. 多媒體
5. **viewpoint** n. 觀點

6. **attend school** 上學
7. **encounter** v. 遭遇
8. **seek** v. 尋求
9. **confine** v. 限制
10. **brainstorm** v. 腦力激盪

Writing Tips

1. 本文依提示先點出一種自己比較喜歡的學習方式，再接著做論述，並舉例來解釋自己偏好此種方式的原因。可用自己目前的學習狀況為藍圖加以延伸說明。同時，也可利用本文的提示來當作文章的開場。

2. 本文常見用法有 some...other... (有些…還有些…)、in the first place (首先) 和 interact with sb (和某人互動)，還有分詞用法 (Studying alone, I'm...)，並適時運用轉折語和副詞，讓文章更流暢，例如：that is、additionally。

78 Choosing a Package Tour

以下為旅行社所安排的兩個旅遊方案：

方案 A：熱帶島嶼渡假勝地 (a tropical island resort)

方案 B：歷史古都遊覽 (a guided tour in a historic town)

如果你有機會免費參與其中一個旅遊方案，你會選擇哪一個？請以此為主題寫一篇英文作文，文分兩段，第一段說明你的選擇與你認為這個行程可能會有的活動，第二段說明你做這個選擇的理由。

　　If I were offered a chance to take one of the tours [1]free of charge, I would choose a tropical island resort tour. This tour would definitely include a stay at a resort with a variety of [2]facilities, such as a swimming pool, a [3]spa, and many restaurants, etc. Also, the resort might be located near a beach where tourists can go [4]canoeing, surfing, and [5]diving. Furthermore, there might be a tropical forest with [6]palm trees nearby for me to go for a [7]stroll.

　　There are two reasons why I would choose a tropical island resort. [8]First of all, I love water sports very much because I come from an island nation. Just to think about the activities I can do, I'm thrilled. Second, I want to take the [9]opportunity to relax and [10]chill out without thinking too much after exams. Therefore, I believe that there's no other tour better than a tropical island resort tour.

Total: 156 words

Vocabulary & Phrases in Use

1. **free of charge** phr. 免費的	6. **palm tree** n. 棕櫚樹
2. **facility** n. 設施	7. **stroll** n. 散步
3. **spa** n. 休閒健康中心	8. **first of all** phr. 首先
4. **canoe** v. 划獨木舟	9. **opportunity** n. 機會
5. **dive** v. 潛水	10. **chill out** phr. 放鬆

Writing Tips

1. 本文論述個人的偏好，須在文章開頭就從兩個選項中選定一個立場，不可語意籠統、含糊不清，也不可兩者都選或兩者都不選。

2. 由於題目是假設性的問題，因此可運用和現在事實相反的假設語氣來描述兩個選項中可能的選擇和此旅遊可能包含的行程內容。第一段用假設語氣 (If I were...)，第二段敘述選擇的理由時，因為是講述事實，則可用現在式。

3. 本文常見用法有 free of charge (免費的)、a variety of facilities (各式各樣的設施) 和 be located... (位於…)，可在類似情境的文章中多加運用。

4. 本文部分內容可套用在描述旅遊計畫、理想中的旅遊景點等類似情境的文章中。

79 The Hobby I Enjoy the Most

請以 "The Hobby I Enjoy the Most" 為主題，寫一篇英文作文，介紹一項你最喜歡從事的嗜好。文分兩段，第一段描述這項嗜好如何進行 (如場地、活動方式、及可能需要的相關用品等)，第二段說明你從事這項嗜好的原因及這項嗜好對你生活的影響。

    The hobby I enjoy the most is cooking at home. I use all kinds of [1]kitchen utensils, such as pots, pans, and knives to make good dishes. Before cooking, I wash vegetables, [2]slice meat, and so on. Then, I can [3]stir fry, boil, or [4]steam them. Following the [5]recipes online, I try to cook [6]yummy and healthy food in my free time.

    As a child, I watched my parents cooking and was always fascinated by the delicious dishes they made. It was under such influence that I showed a great interest in cooking. In fact, cooking at home benefits me and my family. To begin with, homemade dishes not only save a lot of money, but also contain fewer [7]calories and less fat than restaurant food. Furthermore, eating at home helps [8]establish good relations and promotes [9]intimacy among family members. Such an occasion enables me and my family to spend quality time together as each of us talks about what happened during the day. For these two reasons, cooking as a hobby has added spice to my [10]dull life!

Total: 179 words

Vocabulary & Phrases in Use

1. **kitchen utensil** n. 廚具
2. **slice** v. 切
3. **stir fry** v. 炒
4. **steam** v. 蒸
5. **recipe** n. 食譜

6. **yummy** adj. 好吃的
7. **calorie** n. 卡路里
8. **establish** v. 建立
9. **intimacy** n. 親密感
10. **dull** adj. 枯燥乏味的，無趣的

Writing Tips

1. 本文依提示在第一段提出自己最喜歡的嗜好，並介紹此嗜好如何進行，第二段則用過去式稍微回顧自己是在何時為何喜歡上此嗜好，接著詳述此嗜好的優點和對生活造成的正面影響。

2. 可在下筆前先考慮自己的字彙量是否足以詳細描述該嗜好，如果字彙量不足，建議考慮選擇別種嗜好來寫作。

3. 本文常見用法有 be fascinated by sth (著迷於某事) 和 to begin with (首先)，還有分詞 (Following the recipes online, I try...)，以及表示強調的句型 (It was...that...)。

80 English as a Medium of Instruction (110 指考)

近年來，很多大學鼓勵教授以英語講授專業課程，請寫一篇英文作文，說明你對這個現象的看法。文分兩段，第一段說明你是否認同這個趨勢並陳述理由；第二段說明如果你未來就讀的大學必修課是以英語授課，你將會如何因應或規劃。

Nowadays, many colleges in Taiwan encourage their professors to use English as a medium of [2]instruction. I strongly support this program, and the reasons are as follows. Firstly, students' English skills can be improved. Through lectures with English textbooks and [3]communicative activities, students are [4]immersed in an all-English environment. Secondly, this instructional [5]method will attract [6]international students to study in Taiwan. [7]Consequently, we can have better understanding of different cultures and broaden our horizons when we interact with them.

To [8]adapt myself to this change, I need to get fully prepared. Therefore, I will join English clubs to take the chance of using English. Reading English magazines and listening to English programs are also on my to-do list. Besides, whenever possible, I will serve as a volunteer guide for foreigners to practice my speaking skills. Also, I will look up unfamiliar words and [9]terminology in the required in-class readings. Since the lectures are taught in English, it is only with [10]adequate preparation that I can fully [11]absorb the knowledge. In conclusion, I will take advantage of every chance to learn in the courses using English as a medium of instruction, and [12]exert myself to improve my learning both in my professional field and in English.

Total: 205 words

Vocabulary & Phrases in Use

1. **professor** n. 教授
2. **instruction** n. 授課，教導
3. **communicative** adj. 溝通的
4. **immerse** v. 沉浸
5. **method** n. 方法
6. **international** adj. 國際的
7. **consequently** adv. 因此
8. **adapt** v. 使適應
9. **terminology** n. 術語，專門用語
10. **adequate** adj. 足夠的
11. **absorb** v. 吸收
12. **exert oneself** phr. 努力

Writing Tips

1. 在引導式寫作時，應先留意題目要求，依照提示寫作。在表達看法的題型中，必須先表明自己的立場。第一段表態是否認同這個趨勢，並列點說明理由。第二段闡述將會如何因應或規劃，必須提出具體的方式與計畫說明才能得高分。

2. 本文用法多元，例如第一段有表達列舉的 as follows。第二段有動名詞當主詞 (Reading...and listening...are...) ，以及分裂句 it is...that。

167

81 Campus Safety (109 指考)

維護校園安全是校園內每個成員的責任，請寫一篇英文作文，說明應該如何維護校園安全。文分兩段，第一段說明校園安全的重要性及校園內可能發生的安全問題；第二段說明身為校園的一份子，你覺得校內成員應該採取哪些作為以維護校園安全。

There is no denying that a school is the place where students spend most of their time other than their homes. Therefore, a school, in essence, should be a safe place that perform the function of education and provide shelter; it should also be a paradise where students can learn freely and cheerfully. Yet, campus ^{1}safety problems are reported from time to time, including break-ins by ^{2}intruders, unattended playground fatal accidents, or even school ^{3}bullying.

I think that everyone on campus has the responsibility to keep campus safe. For example, schools should check equipment regularly, ^{4}install ^{5}surveillance cameras in blind spots, keep the campus well-lit, and increase police ^{6}patrols to prevent any ^{7}criminal activities. Besides, teachers should be sensitive to students' mental status and create a friendly ^{8}environment. Students can learn to be ^{9}alert and report ^{10}unusual behavior of classmates to their teachers. With the combined efforts, the campus will definitely be a safe and friendly environment for students.

Total: 159 words

Vocabulary & Phrases in Use

1. **safety** n. 安全
2. **intruder** n. 入侵者
3. **bullying** n. 霸凌
4. **install** v. 安裝
5. **surveillance** n. 監視

6. **patrol** n. 巡邏
7. **criminal** adj. 犯罪的
8. **environment** n. 環境
9. **alert** adj. 機警的
10. **unusual** adj. 不尋常的

Writing Tips

1. 在引導式寫作中，務必先留意題目，並依照題目的提示寫作。在發表看法的說明文中，必須提出自己的見解。第一段說明校園安全的重要性，並舉例可能發生的安全問題。第二段說明校內成員應該採取哪些作為以維護校園安全。兩段都是描述事實，時態使用現在式。

2. 本文用法多元，例如第一段有形容詞子句 (...a safe place that perform the function of education and provide shelter)、地方副詞 where 引導的子句 (...a paradise where students can learn freely and cheerfully)，以及第二段有 keep + O + OC (keep the campus well-lit)。

82 The Pride of Taiwan (108 學測)

身為臺灣的一份子，臺灣最讓你感到驕傲的是什麼？請以此為題，寫一篇英文作文，談臺灣最讓你引以為榮的二個面向或事物(例如：人、事、物、文化、制度等)。第一段描述這二個面向或事物，並說明它們為何讓你引以為榮；第二段則說明你認為可以用什麼方式來介紹或行銷這些臺灣特色，讓世人更了解臺灣。

As a Taiwanese, I'm truly proud of my country. Despite having few natural resources, Taiwan has gradually developed many features that make it distinct. The first thing that fills me with ¹pride is our local ²cuisine. Taiwanese have creatively invented various mouth-watering foods, such as beef noodles and bubble tea. These delicious foods not only fill our stomachs but also attract a number of ³tourists. The second feature that makes me proud is our diverse ⁴society. People from different ⁵cultures show respect for one another and live in harmony. For example, south-eastern Asian cuisines have become an essential part of Taiwanese street scenes. While following our own ⁶tradition, we can experience the ⁷customs of other cultures, enriching our lives.

From my ⁸perspective, using social media to ⁹promote Taiwan is an effective method. By taking advantage of social networking websites, like Twitter or Instagram, we can share news, pictures, or stories so that people around the world can learn more about Taiwan. Besides, we can set up a YouTube channel and regularly upload ¹⁰clips to ¹¹advertise different ¹²aspects of Taiwan. Moreover, joining international tourism fairs, such as TBEX and ITB Asia, to

[13]introduce Taiwan is another practical way to let the world know the
[14]beauty of this country!

Total: 207 words

Vocabulary & Phrases in Use

1. **pride** n. 驕傲，自豪
2. **cuisine** n. 料理
3. **tourist** n. 遊客
4. **society** n. 社會
5. **culture** n. 文化
6. **tradition** n. 傳統
7. **custom** n. 習俗

8. **perspective** n. 觀點
9. **promote** v. 行銷，推廣
10. **clip** n. 一段影片
11. **advertise** v. 廣告宣傳
12. **aspect** n. 方面，層面
13. **introduce** v. 介紹
14. **beauty** n. 美好

Writing Tips

1. 在主題寫作時，務必先留意題目，並依照題目的提示寫作。在介紹特色的題型中，要舉出具體例子描述。第一段用到 the first 和 the second 描述二個面向並說明原因。第二段發揮規劃能力闡述如何向世界介紹或行銷臺灣特色。兩段都是描述事實，時態使用現在式。

2. 本篇用法多元，例如第一段有 not only...but also... (not only fill...but also attract...)，以及 while + V-ing (While following...)。第二段用 by + V-ing (By taking advantage of...) 說明可用來行銷臺灣的方式，並用轉折語 besides 與 moreover 來補充資訊。

83 The Queuing Phenomenon (107 學測)

排隊雖是生活中常有的經驗，但我們也常看到民眾一時好奇或基於嘗鮮心理而出現大排長龍 (form a long line) 的現象，例如景點初次開放或媒體介紹某家美食餐廳後，人們便蜂擁而至。請以此種一窩蜂式的「排隊現象」為題，寫一篇英文作文。第一段，以個人、親友的經驗或報導所聞為例，試描述這種排隊情形；第二段，說明自己對此現象的心得或感想。

Recently, a new steakhouse just opened near my house. After the steakhouse was opened, a remarkably long line formed in front of it every day. I was one of the ^{1}customers. On the second day of its opening, my mom and I rushed to the restaurant. Upon arrival, we were surprised by the long line of customers. We ended up spending two hours waiting, during which we witnessed ^{2}disputes due to the ^{3}overcrowded space and people's loss of ^{4}patience. What's worse, the service was poor, and the food was far from satisfactory. Obviously, our waiting in the line was not ^{5}worthwhile at all!

I had a reflection on this experience. ^{6}In my opinion, people tend to follow the crowd blindly without thinking why they want to purchase a product or try some foods. Very often, the ^{7}consequences of this kind of ^{8}bandwagon effect may be regret over their choices and a waste of time and money. Instead of being ^{9}influenced by others, we should consider what appeals to us, look for our favored products, and develop a better understanding of ourselves. ^{10}In conclusion, we should be wise shoppers that shop smart rather than blind followers that waste money and time.

Total: 200 words

Vocabulary & Phrases in Use

1. **customer** n. 顧客
2. **dispute** n. 糾紛
3. **overcrowded** adj. 擁擠不堪的
4. **patience** n. 耐心
5. **worthwhile** adj. 值得的
6. **in one's opinion** phr.
   依某人看來
7. **consequence** n. 後果
8. **bandwagon effect** n.
   從眾效應
9. **influence** v. 影響
10. **in conclusion** phr. 最後

Writing Tips

1. 在主題寫作時，務必先留意題目，並依照題目的提示寫作。在描述現象的題型中，可用故事切入講述主題。第一段用案例描述排隊情形。第二段說明自己的心得或感想。

2. 本篇用法多元，例如第一段有描述時間點的 upon + N/V-ing (Upon arrival,...)，並用 end up 來呈現故事發展 (...ended up spending two hours waiting...)。第二段用 in my opinion 引出自己對一窩蜂式的排隊現象的感想，並延伸說明應該做到的事情，最後以 in conclusion 來總結。

84 Organizing a Community Event (107 指考)

如果你就讀的學校預計辦理一項社區活動，而目前師生初步討論出三個方案：㈠提供社區老人服務 (如送餐、清掃、陪伴等)；㈡舉辦特色市集 (如農產、文創、二手商品等)；㈢舉辦藝文活動 (如展出、表演、比賽等)。這三個方案，你會選擇哪一個？請以此為題，寫一篇英文作文，文長至少 120 個單詞。文分兩段，第一段說明你的選擇及原因，第二段敘述你認為應該要有哪些活動內容，並說明設計理由。

If offered the three [1]options to [2]organize an [3]event for my [4]community, I would choose to organize a [5]fair where people can sell various things. For one thing, it would be beneficial to [6]vendors and customers. For vendors, they can have a good opportunity to [7]display their fresh produce, creative products, or the things they no longer need. As for customers, they can enjoy discounts. For another, I firmly believe that bargains will encourage more [8]interactions and form closer bonds among community [9]residents.

I think the fair should [10]consist of some entertainment activities. For example, we can invite the students from our school clubs to give [11]performances. There can also be a lucky draw game. The more people come, the livelier the atmosphere is. What's more, a fundraising stall would add color to this event. The money received would be sent to the needy, which will better the community. [12]In short, I'm sure this "fun fair" can not only get people out of their homes but also improve the community conditions, in terms of mutual benefit and the relationship among residents.

Total: 181 words

1. **option** n. 選擇，選項

2. **organize** v. 安排，組織

3. **event** n. 活動

4. **community** n. 社區

5. **fair** n. 市集

6. **vendor** n. 攤販；賣家

7. **display** v. 展示，陳列

8. **interaction** n. 互動

9. **resident** n. 居民

10. **consist of** phr. 包含

11. **performance** n. 表演，演出

12. **in short** phr. 總之，簡而言之

1. 在主題寫作時，務必先審題，依照題目的提示寫作。在多選一的題型中，先思考自己決定辦理的活動內容為何，確定後根據此方向發展寫作。

2. 第一段說明選擇為何 ，並善用 for one thing 和 for another 闡述原因。第二段描述要讓這活動成功，應該要包含哪些內容，並具體說明設計理由，可用 for example 來舉例，最後以 in short 總結舉辦此活動有利社區成員並讓社區更美好。

85 My Way to Get Away from Loneliness (106 指考)

每個人從小到大都有覺得寂寞的時刻，也都各自有排解寂寞的經驗和方法。當你感到寂寞時，有什麼人、事或物可以陪伴你，為你排遣寂寞呢？請以此為主題，寫一篇英文作文，文長至少 120 個單詞。文分兩段，第一段說明你會因為什麼原因或在何種情境下感到寂寞，第二段描述某個人、事或物如何伴你度過寂寞時光。

[1]Born into a family of six, I have three [2]siblings and had never known the feeling of [3]loneliness before they went to college. We chatted, played, and fought together. I am grateful for their [4]company. Such a noisy life [5]continued until they all [6]left for college. Since then, I had often felt lonely when I got home. At school, I could chat and play with my classmates. However, when I was home, since my parents often worked long hours, what I could do was to turn on the TV. At that time, I really missed my siblings.

[7]Fortunately, my lonely days didn't last too long. My siblings brought me a small [8]furry kitten when they came home for [9]spring break. They told me that I could have company when they were not home. I was so [10]touched and named the kitten Lara. From then on, this pet cat has lit up my life. Now, the first thing I do after school is not to watch TV, but to look for Lara and play with her.

Total: 175 words

Vocabulary & Phrases in Use

1. **born into** 生於
2. **sibling** n. 手足
3. **loneliness** n. 寂寞
4. **company** n. 陪伴
5. **continue** v. 持續
6. **leave for...** 前往…
7. **fortunately** adv. 幸運地
8. **furry** adj. 毛茸茸的
9. **spring break** n. 春假
10. **touched** adj. 感動的

Writing Tips

1. 本文分為兩段，主要內容分成：(1)說明何種情境下感到寂寞。(2)描述某個人、事或物如何陪伴個人度過寂寞時光。

2. 描寫個人的心境及想法，可多利用表達情緒的形容詞，例如：lonely (寂寞的)、touched (感動的) 以及動詞 feel。

3. 本文常見用法有 since then (從那時起) 和 from then on (從那時起)，還有被動式 (born into)，可在寫作時多加運用。

4. 本文部分內容可套用在描述寵物等類似情境的文章中。

86 What I Think of the Household Chores (105 學測)

你認為家裡生活環境的維持應該是誰的責任?請寫一篇短文說明你的看法。文分兩段,第一段說明你對家事該如何分工的看法及理由,第二段舉例說明你家中家事分工的情形,並描述你自己做家事的經驗及感想。

From my point of view, keeping the home clean and tidy is every family member's responsibility. A family can function well when everyone ¹contributes to the home and ²takes on responsibilities. To share the ³household chores equally and effectively, family members can make a list of things to do together. By doing so, all members will be more ⁴involved and ⁵committed. Besides, parents can ⁶assign tasks to their children or allow them to choose the chores they prefer. Every now and then, the family can have a ⁷discussion to see if anything needs to be ⁸adjusted.

My brother and I have shared the chores since we were little. My parents make doing the household chores a ⁹regular routine. They believe that doing the chores helps build children's ¹⁰character. We started by doing small chores like putting toys away. Now, we have different chores, such as sweeping the floor and doing the laundry. To finish the chores and my homework in a limited time, I've also learned how to manage my time well. All in all, through doing the household chores, I'm delighted to help maintain a clean home and make myself a responsible person at the same time.

Total: 198 words

1. **contribute** v. 貢獻

2. **take on** phr. 承擔 (責任)

3. **household chore** n. 家事

4. **involved** adj. 參與的

5. **committed** adj. 盡心盡力的

6. **assign sth to sb**
   指派某人做某事

7. **discussion** n. 討論

8. **adjust** v. 調整

9. **regular** adj. 規律的

10. **character** n. 品格

1. 本文依提示在第一段先開門見山說明自己認為維持家裡生活環境是誰的責任 (From my point of view...)，接著說明家事該如何分工，並提出理由，第二段舉例說明自己家中家事分工的情形 (My brother and I have shared the chores...)，接著描述本身做家事的經驗及感想，結尾則強調自己做家事的收穫。

2. 本文常見用法有 point of view (想法)、household chore (家事)、build one's character (鍛鍊某人的品格)、in a limited time (在有限的時間內) 和 manage one's time (分配某人的時間)，可在寫作時多加運用。

87 My Opinions on the News and My College Plan (105 指考)

最近有一則新聞報導，標題為「碩士清潔隊員 (waste collectors with a master's degree) 滿街跑」，提及某縣市招考清潔隊員，出現 50 位碩士畢業生報考，引起各界關注。請就這個主題，寫一篇英文作文，文長至少 120 個單詞。文分兩段，第一段依據你的觀察說明這個現象的成因，第二段則就你如何因應上述現象，具體 (舉例) 說明你對大學生涯的學習規劃。

　　The news about 50 applicants with a master's degree competing for a few ¹vacancies for waste collectors has ²hit the headlines. Not only did it become a hot topic, but it also caused public concern. The ³demand from the job market has declined because too many students graduating from college or graduate school every year while not enough vacancies exist. Therefore, these job seekers have difficulty getting ⁴hired, especially when they can't ⁵distinguish themselves from others. It's a good thing they can choose to take blue-collar jobs.

　　To avoid having trouble with job hunting, I will have to prepare myself for future opportunities by making the most of my college life. First, I will take courses in ⁶multiple fields as I believe extensive knowledge is the basic requirement for a good job. Also, I will sharpen my language skills and develop a global perspective by taking language courses and engaging with people from different backgrounds so as to broaden my horizons. What's more, an ⁷internship before graduation will be helpful for my future career.

[8]Equipped with all these skills and knowledge, I'm confident that I will get the job I [9]deserve and that all my efforts will [10]pay off.

Total: 199 words

Vocabulary & Phrases in Use

1. **vacancy** n. 空缺
2. **hit the headlines** phr.
   登上頭條
3. **demand** n. 需求
4. **hire** v. 僱用
5. **distinguish** v. 使有別於

6. **multiple** adj. 多種的
7. **internship** n. 實習
8. **equip** v. 使具備 (能力)
9. **deserve** v. 應得
10. **pay off** phr. 得到好結果

Writing Tips

1. 本文依提示在第一段先說明「碩士清潔隊員滿街跑」的報導引起各界熱議，接著發表看法，並分析這個現象的成因，第二段說明如何規劃大學生涯並提出具體做法，結尾以做好規劃的生涯能夠讓自己利用所學謀得理想職業的信念作為結論。

2. 本文常見用法有 hit the headlines (登上頭條)、sharpen one's language skills (精進某人的語言技能) 和 pay off (得到好結果)，還有 sb will...by V-ing (藉由…某人將…)，可在寫作時多加運用。

88 Reading a Book (104 學測)

下面兩本書是學校建議的暑假閱讀書籍，請依書名想想看該書的
內容，並思考你會選擇哪一本書閱讀，為什麼？請在第一段說明
你會選哪一本書及你認為該書的內容大概會是什麼，第二段提出
你選擇該書的理由。

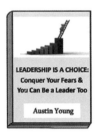

I would choose the book *LEADERSHIP IS A CHOICE: Conquer Your Fears & You Can Be a Leader Too* by Austin Young for my summer reading assignment. As for the [1]content of the book, I [2]suppose that it might [3]revolve around the life experiences of the [4]confident leaders and how they face fears with courage. Then, in the final [5]chapter, I suppose it might include some useful information on how to conquer fears to be a good leader.

I choose this book because I want to be a successful leader. I'm quiet and shy, and I get nervous easily. I admire those who are [6]decisive and [7]competent to guide a group of people. I hope that reading this book can cultivate my mind. I will put what the author [8]conveys into practice. Despite the [9]inner fears and [10]nervousness that trouble me sometimes, I will follow the author's advice to conquer my fears and be a confident leader.

Total: 157 words

Vocabulary & Phrases in Use

1. **content** n. 內容
2. **suppose** v. 猜想，認為
3. **revolve around...** phr. 以…為主題
4. **confident** adj. 自信的
5. **chapter** n. (書的) 章，回
6. **decisive** adj. 果斷的
7. **competent** adj. 有能力的
8. **convey** v. 傳達
9. **inner** adj. 內心的
10. **nervousness** n. 緊張

Writing Tips

1. 本文依提示分為兩段，主要內容分成：⑴選擇哪一本書並猜測書的內容。⑵提出理由與個人觀感。第一段可使用 I would choose the book... 明確提出自己的選擇，接著描寫可能的書籍內容。第二段的第一句 I choose this book because I want to be a successful leader. 直接點明理由，可作為該段的主題句 (topic sentence)，然後再進一步詳細說明。

2. 本文常見用法有 put...into practice (將…付諸實行) 和 follow one's advice (遵循某人的建議)，還有關係代名詞 (I admire those who...)，並適時運用轉折詞，讓文章更流暢，例如：despite。

89 My Experience of Helping Others (104 指考)

指導別人學習讓他學會一件事物，或是得到別人的指導而自己學會一件事物，都是很好的經驗。請根據你過去幫助別人學習，或得到別人的指導而學會某件事的經驗，寫一篇至少 120 個單詞的英文作文。文分兩段，第一段說明該次經驗的緣由、內容和過程，第二段說明你對該次經驗的感想。

Three years ago, I saw an old couple walking [1]hand in hand in my neighborhood with happy smiles on their faces every evening. However, I could only see the old lady alone recently. I hesitated but finally asked her why and learned that her husband had [2]passed away. Seeing the loneliness in her eyes, I decided to make a difference and taught her how to use social media through a smartphone [3]step by step. In the beginning, she considered it [4]complicated and easily [5]dozed off. However, after a while, she found that it was fun to use the Internet. Furthermore, she learned how to use social media to contact her grandchildren abroad. She thanked me with a warm smile that I had not seen [6]for quite a while.

[7]Lying in bed that night, I kept thinking about this experience. It was the first time I plucked up the courage to start a conversation with a [8]stranger. Although she [9]had trouble remembering everything I taught her, we still had a good time together. Moreover, the more I [10]demonstrated, the more interested she became. I felt content and delighted.

Total: 187 words

Vocabulary & Phrases in Use

1. **hand in hand** phr. 手牽手
2. **pass away** phr. 去世
3. **step by step** phr. 逐步地
4. **complicated** adj. 複雜的
5. **doze off** phr. 打瞌睡
6. **for quite a while**
   有很長一段時間
7. **lie in bed** 躺在床上
8. **stranger** n. 陌生人
9. **have trouble + V-ing**
   做…有困難
10. **demonstrate** v. 示範

Writing Tips

1. 本文依提示描寫個人經驗，時態以過去式為主。文分兩段，第一段先鋪陳此經驗的背景與緣由，並陳述經驗內容。第二段說明對於該次經驗的個人感想，最後以助人受益而自己也因此有所收穫作為結尾。

2. 本文常見用法有 make a difference (做出改變) 和 pluck up (the) courage + to V (鼓起勇氣做…)，還有分詞 (Seeing the loneliness in her eyes, I...) 和 the more...the more... (越…越…)，以及加強語氣的用法 (It was the first time I...)，可在寫作時多加運用。

3. 本文部分內容可和第 61 篇 "An Act of Kindness" 互相套用。

⑨ Two Technological Products (102 指考)

以下有兩項即將上市之新科技產品：

產品一：隱形披風
(invisibility cloak)

穿上後頓時隱形，旁人看不到你的存在；同時，隱形披風會保護你，讓你水火不侵。

產品二：智慧型眼鏡
(smart glasses)

具有掃描透視功能，戴上後即能看到障礙物後方的生物；同時能完整紀錄你所經歷過的場景。

如果你有機會獲贈其中一項產品，你會選擇哪一項？請以此為主題，寫一篇至少 120 個單詞的英文作文。文分兩段，第一段說明你的選擇及理由，並舉例說明你將如何使用這項產品。第二段說明你不選擇另一項產品的理由及該項產品可能衍生的問題。

If given a chance to receive one of these two [1]technological products, I would choose the invisibility cloak. I can use this cloak to keep myself from being seen whenever I [2]am caught up in dangerous or embarrassing situations. Moreover, since this cloak is both [3]waterproof and [4]fireproof, it can keep me from any harm if I'm caught in flood or on fire. Furthermore, I can also use this cloak to save those who are [5]threatened with [6]robberies or fire.

[7]Compared with the invisibility cloak, the smart glasses appear less fascinating to me. Since one of its two [8]functions is to see through things, I'm worried that I may accidentally [9]invade other people's privacy. The other function of recording may trouble me as

well. What if I don't want to record all the bad things in life? Out of these [10]concerns, I would definitely choose the invisibility cloak.

Total: 148 words

Vocabulary & Phrases in Use

1. **technological** adj. 科技的
2. **be caught up in** phr. 陷入
3. **waterproof** adj. 防水的
4. **fireproof** adj. 防火的
5. **threaten** v. 威脅
6. **robbery** n. 搶劫
7. **compare** v. 比較
8. **function** n. 作用
9. **invade** v. 侵犯
10. **concern** n. 擔憂

Writing Tips

1. 本文依提示分為兩段，第一段說明個人選擇及理由，並舉例說明將如何使用這項產品，第二段說明不選擇另一項產品的原因及該項產品可能衍生的問題。

2. 可在下筆前先考慮自己的字彙量，並評估自己比較有把握說明哪一種產品，再決定寫作的內容。

3. 本文常見用法有 be caught up in (陷入 ， 被捲入) 和 keep sb from sth (使某人免遭受某事) ，還有假設語氣 (if...) 和分詞 (Compared with..., the smart glasses appear...)。

⑨ Doing Exercise (101 指考)

請以運動為主題，寫一篇至少 120 個單詞的文章，說明你最常從事的運動是什麼。文分兩段，第一段描述這項運動如何進行 (如地點、活動方式、及可能需要的相關用品等)，第二段說明你從事這項運動的原因及這項運動對你生活的影響。

[1]Cycling, one of my favorite sports, is suitable for people of different ages and groups. To do this sport, apart from the [2]indispensable bicycle, a rider may need some sports [3]gear, such as a [4]helmet to [5]prevent harm to the head, a pair of gloves to keep hands comfortable, and sunglasses to protect eyes from the sun. Whoever feels like [6]stretching the [7]muscles can go cycling anytime and anywhere. What's more, it can be done by oneself or with others.

There are some reasons why I'm interested in cycling. First, it improves my [8]fitness, refreshes my mind, and relieves my tension. Besides, I can enjoy beautiful views while cycling, [9]particularly in the mountains. Last, I [10]am fond of riding a bicycle with my good friends. To sum up, cycling benefits me physically and mentally.

Total: 134 words

Vocabulary & Phrases in Use

1. **cycling** n. 騎腳踏車
2. **indispensable** adj. 不可或缺的
3. **gear** n. 裝備
4. **helmet** n. 安全帽
5. **prevent** v. 預防
6. **stretch** v. 伸展
7. **muscle** n. 肌肉
8. **fitness** n. 健康
9. **particularly** adv. 特別地
10. **be fond of** phr. 喜愛

Writing Tips

1. 本文依提示分為兩段，第一段描述個人常從事的運動如何進行及相關的物品，第二段說明喜歡這項運動的原因與好處，時態多以現在式為主。

2. 可在下筆前先考慮自己的字彙量是否足以描述某項運動及其所需之配備，藉此評估要選擇描述哪一項運動。寫作此類文章時，游泳、騎腳踏車或跑步通常比登山或溯溪更容易發揮。

3. 本文常見用法有 be interested in (有興趣)、improve one's fitness (改善某人的健康)、relieve one's tension (舒緩某人的緊張) 和 be fond of (喜愛)，可在類似情境的文章中多加運用。

4. 本文中的 stretch the muscles、improve one's fitness、refresh one's mind、relieve one's tension 等用法，可套用在描述各種運動或討論運動好處等類似情境的文章中。

92 A Graduation Ceremony (100 指考)

你認為畢業典禮應該是個溫馨感人、活潑熱鬧、或是嚴肅傷感的場景？請寫一篇英文作文說明你對畢業典禮的看法，第一段寫出畢業典禮對你而言意義是什麼，第二段說明要如何安排或進行活動才能呈現出這個意義。

A graduation ceremony is an event of great ¹significance. For me, it not only ²symbolizes the end of my three-year studies, but also represents a ³milestone in my life. Moreover, the ceremony can help me look back on the past years during which I've spent happy days with my ⁴fellow students. At the same time, it inspires me to look forward to the future.

Since this ceremony is dedicated to the graduates, it should have a ⁵theme that ⁶involves all the graduates. Furthermore, all the ⁷decorations and costumes for that day should be based on the theme as well. Besides, to make this happy and touching ceremony meaningful, graduates can invite the ⁸principal, teachers, and parents to give them ⁹blessings. What's more, they can have a ¹⁰slide show as a reminder of their happy memories during high school years. In conclusion, graduates should take this ceremony seriously and make it as meaningful as possible.

Total: 154 words

Vocabulary & Phrases in Use

1. **significance** n. 重要性
2. **symbolize** v. 象徵
3. **milestone** n. 里程碑
4. **fellow** adj. 同伴的
5. **theme** n. 主題

6. **involve** v. 包含
7. **decoration** n. 裝飾
8. **principal** n. 校長
9. **blessing** n. 祝福
10. **slide show** n. 幻燈片放映

Writing Tips

1. 本文依提示在第一段說明對自己而言畢業典禮有何意義,描述事實使用現在式時態即可,第二段承接上一段所說的意義,詳細說明典禮應如何進行,例如利用主題、邀請師長給予祝福、播放幻燈片等,使用現在式時態比較恰當。

2. 本文常見用法有 represent a milestone (代表一個里程碑)、look back (回顧) 以及 look forward to (盼望),並適時運用副詞和片語,讓文章更流暢,例如:besides 和 what's more。

93 Smell and Memory (99 指考)

在你的記憶中，哪一種氣味 (smell) 最讓你難忘？請寫一篇英文作文，文長至少 120 字，文分兩段，第一段描述你在何種情境中聞到這種氣味，以及你初聞這種氣味時的感受，第二段描述這個氣味至今仍令你難忘的理由。

I can't forget the smell of the hospital. When I was a junior high school student, one day, my best friend, Sean, was sent to the hospital after a serious car accident. He spent many days in the [1]intensive care unit, and he couldn't talk because [2]he was hooked up to a [3]breathing machine. How poor Sean was! He had no choice but to lie still [4]all day. Therefore, I kept talking to him and tried to make him feel comfortable when I was there. The hospital smelled of [5]disinfectant or [6]bleach, making me feel worried and nervous. Fortunately, he recovered from his illness after a month. At that moment, his family and I couldn't help but cry with joy.

[7]As time goes by, my memory [8]fades. However, the smell of the hospital is clear and [9]distinct. To this day, whenever I go to the hospital, I still can't ignore the unforgettable smell. That hospital smell always reminds me of how anxious I was when my best friend [10]suffered in the hospital.

Total: 172 words

Vocabulary & Phrases in Use

1. **intensive care unit** n. (abbr. ICU) 加護病房
2. **sb be hooked up to...** 將…接到某人身上
3. **breathing machine** n. 呼吸器
4. **all day** 整天
5. **disinfectant** n. 消毒劑
6. **bleach** n. 漂白劑
7. **as time goes by** 隨著時間流逝
8. **fade** v. (記憶) 逐漸消逝
9. **distinct** adj. 明顯的
10. **suffer** v. 受苦

Writing Tips

1. 本文依提示在第一段以一個故事描述初次聞到某個氣味時的情景及感受，使用過去式時態，第二段以氣味與人的情感連結，來說明此氣味令自己難忘的原因。若要精確描述氣味，需要比較大量的字彙，因此以故事的方式來描述會比較容易。

2. 本文常見用法有 have no choice but + to V (不得不…)、can't help but + V (不禁…) 和 as time goes by (隨著時間流逝)，並適時運用時間副詞，讓文章更流暢，例如：at that moment、to this day。

94 How to Spend My Day with No Budget Limit (98 指考)

如果你可以不用擔心預算，隨心所欲的度過一天，你會怎麼過？
請寫一篇短文，第一段說明你會邀請誰和你一起過這一天？為
什麼？第二段描述你會去哪裡？做些什麼事？為什麼？

Without worrying about the ¹budget, I would take my time comfortably and have a ²leisurely one-day trip with my younger sister, Ellen. ³For one thing, I've ⁴longed to take a trip with her, and for another, I can treat her to any luxuries without concerns of budget. Going out with her makes me feel warm because she is a caring and ⁵warm-hearted sister.

I wish we could go to Beitou for a day trip because it is famous for its hot springs. We would travel by taxi. ⁶The following is our ⁷itinerary. In the morning, we would explore nature and watch ⁸wildlife in the mountains. At noon, we would enjoy a five-course meal at a high-class restaurant of a five-star hotel. After lunch, we would enjoy ourselves in a ⁹luxurious hot spring hotel. In the evening, we would admire the ¹⁰night view of city from the top of a grand hotel, having cool drinks. In conclusion, if I could spend a day without worrying about the budget, I would take a day trip to Beitou with my dearest sister.

Total: 179 words

Vocabulary & Phrases in Use

1. **budget** n. 預算
2. **leisurely** adj. 悠閒的
3. **for one thing..., and for another...** phr.
   一方面…，另一方面…
4. **long to V** 渴望…
5. **warm-hearted** adj. 熱心的
6. **the following** phr. 下列
7. **itinerary** n. 行程
8. **wildlife** n. 野生動物
9. **luxurious** adj. 奢華的
10. **night view** n. 夜景

Writing Tips

1. 本文依提示在第一段說明如果不用擔心預算的情況下，個人會邀請誰一起度過一天並說明理由，第二段描述想去哪裡、做些什麼事以及理由。須注意時態的變化，陳述事實使用現在式時態，假設語氣則使用 would 搭配原形動詞。

2. 本文部分內容可套用在敘述未來的旅遊計畫、想去的地方、畢業旅行或最想做的一件事等類似情境的文章中。

3. 本文常見用法有 be famous for... (以…聞名的) 和 the following is... (下列是…)，還有假設語氣 (if...)，可在寫作時多加運用。

95 A Commercial (97 指考)

廣告在我們生活中隨處可見。請寫一篇大約 120–150 字的短文，
介紹一則令你印象深刻的電視或平面廣告。第一段描述該廣告的
內容 (如：主題、故事情節、音樂、畫面等)，第二段說明該廣告
令你印象深刻的原因。

    The TV [1]commercial that impresses me most is the one for a
[2]brand of [3]canned coffee called Mr. Brown Coffee. This brand of
coffee bears a logo [4]recognized by many people. In the TV
commercial, the beautiful view of the countryside really catches my
eye. There is one scene where four girls have a good time together,
and each of them holds a can of Mr. Brown Coffee happily. Another
scene shows that many people camp [5]overnight in a field cheerfully,
and each with a can of Mr. Brown Coffee, too.

    The Mr. Brown Coffee commercial is so [6]impressive because
of the [7]catchy [8]jingle and the people's happy faces when they have
the [9]beverage beside them. It seems that as long as people hold a can
of Mr. Brown Coffee in their hands, they feel satisfied and
contented. Additionally, people even enjoy one another's company
more since they all drink the same brand of coffee. In conclusion,
the Mr. Brown Coffee commercial impresses me, a potential
[10]consumer, most.

Total: 168 words

Vocabulary & Phrases in Use

1. **commercial** n. 廣告
2. **brand** n. 品牌
3. **canned** adj. 罐裝的
4. **recognize** v. 認出
5. **overnight** adv. 整夜
6. **impressive** adj.
   令人印象深刻的

7. **catchy** adj. 琅琅上口的
8. **jingle** n. 廣告歌
9. **beverage** n. 飲料
10. **consumer** n. 消費者

Writing Tips

1. 本文依提示在第一段描述令自己印象深刻的廣告內容，第二段說明該廣告令人印象深刻的原因，全文可使用現在簡單式代表描述一項客觀的事實。

2. 可在下筆前先考慮自己的字彙量是否足以描述廣告內容，藉此評估要選擇描述哪一則廣告。建議平時可先準備相關內容，寫作時才好發揮。

3. 本文常見用法有 called (叫做)、catch one's eye (引起某人的注意) 和 as long as (只要)，並適時運用轉折語，讓文章更流暢，例如：additionally。

⑨6 Travel Is The Best Teacher (93 指考)

請以 "Travel Is The Best Teacher" 為主題，寫一篇至少 120 個字的英文作文。第一段針對文章主題，說明旅行的優點，並在第二段舉自己在國內或國外的旅行經驗，以印證第一段的說明。

　　Travel plays an important part in my life. It is a good way to relieve my tension. Besides, when I go traveling, I always see and learn something new. That is, travel serves not only as a ¹pastime, but also as the best teacher.

　　Last year, I took a trip to Japan with my older brother and learned a valuable lesson. On my first day in Japan, I was so hungry that I ate some snacks while I was walking on the street. ²All of a sudden, a Japanese came to me and said something in Japanese. Through my brother's ³translation, I learned that the Japanese ⁴generally don't eat while walking. Such behavior may leave the street ⁵littered with trash and trouble the passers-by. Looking around the tidy ⁶surroundings, I ⁷was impressed by how ⁸organized the Japanese were. To them, everyone is ⁹responsible for keeping the streets clean. Therefore, any ¹⁰self-centered behavior would not be allowed. After this event, I have become more aware of other people's thoughts and the environment. Thus, travel is the best teacher, for it helps me to experience and learn new things.

Total: 187 words

Vocabulary & Phrases in Use

1. **pastime** n. 消遣活動
2. **all of a sudden** phr. 突然
3. **translation** n. 翻譯
4. **generally** adv. 普遍地
5. **litter** v. 亂丟 (垃圾)
6. **surroundings** n. 環境
7. **be impressed by...**
   對⋯印象深刻
8. **organized** adj. 有條理的
9. **responsible** adj. 有責任的
10. **self-centered** adj. 自我中心的

Writing Tips

1. 本文依提示分為兩段，主要內容分成：⑴說明旅行的優點。⑵描述旅行的經驗。第一段說明旅行的優點，為陳述個人的想法，使用現在式時態，並且在最後一句將本文主旨點出。第二段描述過去的旅行經驗，所以多用過去式時態。結尾陳述個人的感想，則使用現在式時態。

2. 本文常見用法有 relieve one's tension (舒緩某人的緊張) 、 take a trip to...with sb (和某人去⋯旅行) 和 be impressed by... (對⋯印象深刻)，還有分詞用法 (Looking around the tidy surroundings, I...)，可在寫作時多加運用。

3. 本文部分內容可套用在談論國際及跨文化經驗等類似情境的文章中。

97 Exams (92 指考)

小考、段考、複習考、畢業考、甚至校外其他各種大大小小的考試，已成為高中學生生活中不可或缺的一部分。請寫一篇 120 至 150 個單詞左右的英文作文，文分兩段，第一段以 Exams of all kinds have become a necessary part of my high school life. 為主題句；第二段則以 The most unforgettable exam I have ever taken is... 為開頭並加以發展。

Exams of all kinds have become a [1]necessary part of my high school life. [2]In my case, I have at least three quizzes every day. [3]Overwhelmed by the heavy schoolwork, I can't help wondering the meaning of exams sometimes. [4]Nonetheless, I learned a [5]crucial lesson through exam [6]preparation.

The most unforgettable exam I have ever taken is a [7]weekly English test in my first high school year. Not having prepared for it at all, I couldn't answer any of the questions and failed it. When my teacher, Ms. Chen, saw my poor grade, she didn't [8]blame me for [9]flunking the test. Instead, she asked me what had happened and realized that I had been too busy with my extracurricular activities to study. After she knew of my situation, she sat down and taught me how to manage my time properly. I followed her advice and [10]got my priorities right in my life. My grades improved, and I also became a club leader. I really appreciated the precious lesson my teacher taught me. Best of all, the exams have never been a problem for me since then.

Total: 186 words

Vocabulary & Phrases in Use

1. **necessary** adj. 必需的
2. **in...case** phr. 在…情況下
3. **overwhelm** v. 壓垮
4. **nonetheless** adv. 儘管如此
5. **crucial** adj. 至關重要的
6. **preparation** n. 準備
7. **weekly** adj. 每週的
8. **blame** v. 責怪
9. **flunk** v. (考試) 不及格
10. **get one's priorities right** phr. 分清事情的輕重緩急

Writing Tips

1. 本文依提示分為兩段，主要內容分成：(1)對考試的想法。(2)令人難忘的考試經驗。第一段陳述個人想法，多用現在式時態，第二段講述個人經驗則多用過去式時態。

2. 本文常見用法有 can't help + V-ing (不禁…)、learn a crucial lesson through... (藉由…學到重要的一課) 和 extracurricular activity (課外活動)，還有分詞用法 (Overwhelmed by..., I can't help...)，並適時運用轉折語和副詞，使文章更流暢，例如：nonetheless 和 instead。

3. 本文部分內容可套用在描述學到寶貴的教訓等類似情境的文章中；另外，本文第二段的部分內容可套用在第 60 篇 "An Unforgettable Teacher" 文章中。

⑱ The Most Precious Thing in My Room (91 學測)

以 "The Most Precious Thing in My Room" 為題寫一篇英文作文，描述你的房間內一件你最珍愛的物品，同時並說明珍愛的理由。(這一件你最珍愛的物品不一定是貴重的，但對你來說卻是最有意義或是最值得紀念的。)

    The most precious thing in my room is a [1]wooden [2]boomerang, a [3]typical [4]souvenir of Australia. When I was a junior high school student, I went to Brisbane for a one-month [5]study tour in summer. It was my first time to live with an Australian homestay family and learn their customs. Although I felt [6]homesick at first, my [7]host family treated me like one of their own family. Whenever they had free time, they took me to many interesting spots. They also took me to the park and threw the boomerang very often. One month later, when I was about to go back to Taiwan, the host family gave me a wooden boomerang. However, it was not just any boomerang, but the boomerang that we used in the park. They wanted me to think of them whenever I saw it. At that moment, I couldn't help but [8]burst out crying and gave them a [9]hearty hug.

    Now, it is on my desk in my room. Whenever I see it, it brings back many happy memories of my sweet and [10]hospitable host family in Australia. In conclusion, my wooden boomerang is the most precious thing in my room.

Total: 197 words

Vocabulary & Phrases in Use

1. **wooden** adj. 木製的
2. **boomerang** n. 回力棒
3. **typical** adj. 典型的
4. **souvenir** n. 紀念品
5. **study tour** n. 遊學
6. **homesick** adj. 想家的
7. **host family** n. 寄宿家庭
8. **burst out crying** phr.
   突然大哭
9. **hearty** adj. 熱情的
10. **hospitable** adj. 熱情友好的

Writing Tips

1. 本文分為兩段，主要內容分成：(1)房間中最珍愛的物品及該物品的
   故事。(2)珍愛的理由。時態依文章內容而變化，描述過去經驗時以
   過去式時態為主，談到珍愛的理由時，以現在式時態為主。

2. 本文常見用法有 treat sb like... (對待某人像是⋯)、can't help but +
   V (不禁⋯) 和 give sb a hearty hug (熱情地擁抱某人)，並適時運用
   連接詞，讓文章更流暢，例如：although 和 whenever。

3. 本文部分內容可套用在描述國外旅遊經驗、跨文化的國際經驗或接
   受過最喜歡或最有紀念價值的禮物等類似情境的文章中。

203

99 If I Won Two Million Dollars in the Lottery (91 指考)

文章請以 "If I won two million dollars in the lottery, I would help..." 開始，敘述如果你或妳贏得臺灣樂透彩新臺幣兩百萬元之後，最想把全數金額拿去幫助的人、機構或組織，並寫出理由。

If I won two million dollars in the [1]lottery, I would help the teenagers in the countryside to learn music. As a young [2]musician, I truly believe that music can make one's [3]youth colorful.

I was born and raised in the countryside. In such [4]remote areas, the living standards and [5]educational resources may not be as good as those in the [6]urban areas. Fortunately, I met a great music teacher, Mr. Tsai, in school. He was a cool guy and introduced a wide variety of music to us. Under his instruction, I started learning the piano and also writing [7]lyrics. After a few months, my family members were so impressed with my beautiful piano playing. Now, I'm an [8]outstanding musician, and I'm grateful to have the opportunity to enjoy a wide range of music. Music helps me adopt a [9]positive attitude toward my life. Therefore, if I won the lottery, I would like to spend the money on building music classrooms in the countryside, where I can help cultivate teenagers' musical [10]talent.

Total: 172 words

1. **lottery** n. 樂透
2. **musician** n. 音樂家
3. **youth** n. 青年時期
4. **remote** adj. 偏遠的
5. **educational resources** n. 教育資源
6. **urban** adj. 都市的
7. **lyric** n. 歌詞
8. **outstanding** adj. 傑出的
9. **positive** adj. 正面的
10. **talent** n. 才能

Writing Tips

1. 本文分為兩段，主要內容分成：(1)想捐助的對象。(2)捐助的理由。第一段第一句以「與現在事實相反」的假設語氣，寫出想要捐助的對象。第二段以實際明確的例子來說明這個對象為什麼需要這筆捐款的幫助。文章結尾可再重述一次這項決定，以加強讀者的印象。

2. 本文常見用法有 living standards (生活水準)、a wide variety of (各式各樣的)、under one's instruction (在某人的指導下) 和 a wide range of (各式各樣的)，還有假設語氣 (If I won..., I would help...)，可在寫作時多加運用。

3. 本文部分內容可套用在探討改善成長環境等類似情境的文章中。

100 Something Interesting about a Classmate of Mine (90 學測)

請以 "Something Interesting about a Classmate of Mine" 為題，寫出有關你一位同學的一件趣事。這位同學可以是你任何時期的同學，例如中學、小學或幼稚園的同學。

Nick was one of my high school classmates. He barely said a word in class, so all the teachers and other classmates found it difficult to communicate with him. However, [1]little by little, we found Nick was actually an interesting guy, and we could communicate a lot with him by writing words on paper.

We [2]got used to this kind of communication with Nick and almost forgot that he could "speak." One day, in our senior year, all the students were invited to a [3]campus [4]karaoke competition. As we were wondering where Nick was, we saw him holding a [5]microphone on stage and singing a popular rap like a superstar. This scene made all of us [6]speechless at first, but soon we [7]cheered and [8]clapped our hands in [9]excitement. That was the first time I heard Nick's clear and charming voice. [10]Needless to say, Nick won the competition that day. From then on, this event has been [11]brought up over and over again among all the classmates as it is the most interesting thing that happened in our high school years.

Total: 181 words

Vocabulary & Phrases in Use

1. **little by little** phr. 漸漸地
2. **get used to...** phr. 習慣於…
3. **campus** n. 校園
4. **karaoke competition** n.
   卡拉 OK 比賽
5. **microphone** n. 麥克風

6. **speechless** adj. 說不出話來的
7. **cheer** v. 歡呼
8. **clap one's hands** 鼓掌
9. **excitement** n. 興奮
10. **needless to say** phr. 不用說
11. **bring up** phr. 提出

Writing Tips

1. 本文依提示描述一位同學發生過的「一件趣事」，以過去式時態為
   主。
2. 本文常見用法有 get used to... (習慣於…)、one day (有一天) 和 the
   first time (初次) ，並適時運用慣用語 ，讓文章更流暢 ，例如：
   needless to say。
3. 本文部分內容可套用在描述一位朋友或是求學時發生過的一件趣
   事等類似情境的文章中。

英語 *Make Me High* 系列

作文 100 隨身讀

彙　　　整	三民英語編輯小組
插畫設計	李昊宏
發 行 人	劉振強
出 版 者	三民書局股份有限公司
地　　　址	臺北市復興北路 386 號 (復北門市)
	臺北市重慶南路一段 61 號 (重南門市)
電　　　話	(02)25006600
網　　　址	三民網路書店 https://www.sanmin.com.tw
出版日期	初版一刷 2009 年 4 月
	四版一刷 2022 年 11 月
書籍編號	S807890
I S B N	978-957-14-7517-2

20分鐘稱霸
大考英文作文

王靖賢 編著

- ・共16回作文練習,涵蓋大考作文3大題型: 看圖寫作、主題寫作、信函寫作。根據近年 大考趨勢精心出題,題型多元且擬真度高。
- ・每回作文練習皆有為考生精選的英文名言佳 句,增強考生備考戰力。
- ・附方便攜帶的解析本,針對每回作文題目提 供寫作架構圖,讓寫作脈絡一目了然,並提 供範文、寫作要點、寫作撇步及好用詞彙, 一本在手即可增強英文作文能力。

大考英文
字彙力6000
隨身讀

三民英語編輯小組　彙整

第一本完整收錄最新字表的隨身讀！
獨家贈送「拼讀」音檔，用聽的也能背單字！

◆ 收錄最新字表完整內容！
　參照108新課綱「高中英文參考詞彙表(111
　學年度起適用)」彙整，全面提升大考英文
　字彙力。

◆ 獨家贈送「拼讀」音檔，讓你用聽的就能把
　單字背起來！
　音檔採拼讀模式(success，s-u-c-c-e-s-s，
　success，成功)；並由專業外籍錄音員錄
　製，用準確的發音記憶字彙。

◆ 補充詳盡！
　常用搭配詞、介系詞、同反義字及片語等各
　項補充豐富。

神拿滿級分——
英文學測總複習
（二版）

孫至娟　編著

新型學測總複習必備！
十回十足準備，滿級分手到擒來！

● 重點搭配練習：
　　雙效合一有感複習，讓你應試力UP！
● 議題式心智圖：
　　補充時事議題單字，讓你單字力UP！
● 文章主題多元：
　　符合學測多元取材，讓你閱讀力UP！
● 混合題最素養：
　　多樣混合題型訓練，讓你理解力UP！
● 獨立作文頁面：
　　作答空間超好運用，讓你寫作力UP！
● 詳盡解析考點：
　　見題拆題精闢解析，讓你解題力UP！